HOW TO
CATCH CLAMS
BY THE BUSHEL!

HOW TO CATCH CLAMS BY THE BUSHEL!

By Tom Schlichter

**Illustrations by
Vincent Piazza**

**NORTHEAST SPORTSMAN'S PRESS
TARRYTOWN, NEW YORK**

**STACKPOLE BOOKS
HARRISBURG, PENNSYLVANIA**

Library of Congress Cataloging in Publication Data
Schlichter, Tom
  How to catch clams by the bushel! / by Tom Schlichter : drawings
by Vincent Piazza
     p.   cm.
   ISBN 0-8117-4020-X : $8.95
   1. Clamming — United States. 2. Shellfish gathering — United
States. 3. Cookery (Shellfish) I. Title.
   SH400.5.C53S35 1990
   799.2 540973—dc20

                                      89—26643
                                        CIP

Most of the recipes in this book were created, compiled and tested with the generous assistance of Tina Schlichter. Additional recipes were submitted by Victoria O'Conner and Mike Tancredi.

Published by Stackpole Books and Northeast Sportsman's Press
Distributed by Stackpole Books
Cameron & Kelker Streets
Harrisburg, Pennsylvania 17105

Printed in the United States of America
10-9-8-7-6-5-4-3-2-1

ACKNOWLEDGEMENTS

Like many outdoor books, this one started off as a simple idea the author thought he could tackle himself. I quickly found, however, that there was an amazing amount to learn about shellfishing up and down the coast — even for someone who has been clamming since childhood. I must admit, then, that I had a great deal of expert help in refining this text.

One resource on which I heavily relied is the coastal network of Sea Grant Specialists and Cornell Cooperative Extension Agents. These two agencies provided me with reams of shellfish literature, often on short notice. Especially helpful were Gregg Rivara, a Cornell Cooperative Extension Agent in Suffolk Co., NY, who checked much of the text for accuracy, and Ken Gall, Seafood Specialist for NY Sea Grant, who provided expert advice on storing, cleaning and preparing the catch.

For his timely advice and expert editing of the text, Jim Capossela also deserves a pat on the back.

Others who contributed in significant ways included Matt Martin, Burke's Fish Store in East Moriches, NY, The Fish Store in Bayport, NY, and various state and town shellfishing bureaus.

Finally, I would like to thank my wife Tina, who helped research and write the recipe chapter, and my daughters Corrine and Lauren, who endured a summer of endless photo sessions as we bounced from beach to beach. Next year girls, I'll put away the camera and we'll just concentrate on filling our baskets and having fun.

To my wife
Tina,
and daughters
Corrine and Lauren,
with whom I hope to share many more fun-filled days
combing beaches of every kind.

CONTENTS

IMPORTANT NOTE ON SHELLFISHING SAFETY AND REGULATIONS

*A*s with any other outdoor sport, certain rules apply to shellfishing which can't be overlooked. For your own safety, and that of your loved ones, be a stickler for proper procedure whenever you choose to harvest a meal from the sea.

To start with, purchase the proper licenses or permits and shellfish only in waters that have been "certified" as clean by your local shellfish commission, bureau or agency. Never gather clams, oysters, mussels, scallops, whelks, snails, or any other creature to be consumed, from waters that appear polluted in any way. Note, too, that pollution isn't always visible to the naked eye; runoff from farms and houses may infiltrate what otherwise appears to be a pristine stretch of beach and, in some areas, toxic algae blooms can contaminate shellfish making them unfit for human consumption. In either instance, no visible signs may be present to cue you in. If you aren't sure that a particular stretch of beach is open for public shellfishing, call your shellfish agency and ask. If you still aren't sure, skip it and move onto some area that is better marked.

Most every state, county and town has a set of shellfishing regulations, a copy of which should be provided with your license or permit. Read up on the current rules and take nothing for granted. These stipulations are designed to protect shellfish stocks from overharvesting and the shellfisherman from corraling a tainted meal. In most jurisdictions the rules are strictly enforced. Tickets and fines await violators.

Before you head home with catch in hand, and again before you serve them up, check each and every morsel to ensure it is clean and healthy looking. Shellfish which have died should never be eaten. Neither should any which smell foul or appear disfigured. A simple rule of thumb applies to eating all types of shellfish: *When in doubt, don't.* It's far better to discard an entire day's catch than risk becoming ill. You wouldn't eat a mushroom you were unsure of, would you?

While out collecting your meal, be certain to wear appropriate clothing — gloves and footwear are necessary items for catching any shellfish species in any kind of environment. A cap, sunglasses, shirt, sun screen or diver's wet suit may also be appropriate at times.

Finally, keep a close eye on the kids. Jetties, slippery rock strewn shores and grassy, mud bottomed marshes all present obvious challenges but even a sandy white beach can subtly hide deep water and strong currents lurking nearby. Best to check it out before turning the kids loose.

Before you head out to join the fun, please read thoroughly the following chapters. Especially important from a safety standpoint are Chapter 6, "Finding Shellfish Beds" and Chapter 7, "Cleaning and Storing Your Catch". Many other safety hints are offered throughout the text as they apply.

One

THE BEAUTY OF SHELLFISHING

*W*hat is it that makes the catching of such simple creatures as clams, mussels and oysters so alluring? The answers can be pleasingly diverse, as each clammer has his or her own reasons for heading to the shore.

Certainly at the top of the list is the thought of a fresh and tasty meal. It's been said that it was a brave person who first ate an oyster, and that's probably true. But since that first genius survived the occasion, millions of others have given it a try and, finding the experience wholly pleasurable, proceeded to gulp down also hard and softshell clams, mussels, conch, periwinkles, and even, most recently, barnacles. While it still takes a stiff upper lip to swallow that first-ever raw shellfish, those that follow are often considered to be pure delight.

Although it doesn't quite have the broad appeal of baseball or apple pie, clamming is arguably a great American pastime, at least along the coast. And why shouldn't it be? Everybody loves a bargain and shellfish are free. Americans today are concerned with healthy eating and shellfish are nutritious, low in fat and low in cholesterol. Time to travel is a luxury not everyone can afford and shellfish are readily available close to home, providing a great reason to escape without mandating a long and tiring roadtrip. "What about exercise?" you may inquire. Well, to be truthful, I've never seen a clam do push-ups but I can guarantee *you'll* get a workout trying to catch them. Forget the fact that most shellfish are slow moving; simply bending over a couple hundred times each trip is more than some people exert themselves in a week at home. And, as any veteran shellfisherman can attest, some kinds of shellfish can move quickly while others are quite capable of resisting your most determined tugs and pryings.

Be it known also that clamming is *fun!* There's just something very satisfying about catching your own dinner, especially when the eats are bound to be delicious. Somehow, it transcends our basic instincts to hunt and fish, combining these two favorite pastimes in a unique way that allows for almost inevitable success while still presenting a daily challenge. Furthermore, almost anyone can go clamming. Parents, children, even grandparents can participate if they like. All that's needed is a little know-how, determination and, of course, suitable waters. Clamming is the perfect, low cost and rewarding activity to try on vacation, whether you visit Cape Cod, Cape Hatteras or any one of a thousand other beaches.

For some of us, the desire to shellfish stems partially from frugality. Why pay $4.00 for a dozen hard clams when you can go to the shore and pick

them yourself? Mussels and steamer clams, though only a buck or two a pound at the fish market, are free for the taking at most beaches. Oysters and scallops, often downright expensive, are less common in some areas but still widespread enough that most coastal residents can scrounge up a few. (Truth be known, though, once hooked on clamming you'll still find yourself going to the fish market to buy your meals when you can't get down to the beach. This is especially so during the cold winter months. You might even buy more shellfish than before once they've become a staple in your diet.)

All of the shellfish covered in this book can be gathered by hand, which means there are no start up costs to clamming, save for the possible purchase of an inexpensive license in some areas. For the more industrious, specialized rakes, pitchforks, shovels, and tongs can be bought or fashioned. Now there's even a way to suck your quarry from its subterranean home with a simple mechanical aid. And once you've cheaply filled your basket with enough to start a meal, you'll revel in finding that shellfish lend themselves well to a myriad of cooking methods. Some kinds are even eaten raw, their delicate, natural taste putting most "recipes" to shame.

My own start in clamming came from necessity. I raked hard clams commercially to help pay college tuition. Of course, I must admit that there were other jobs available, some higher paying and less dependent on clear weather, but none of those would allow me to get out on the water each and every day. Recalling the time, it was backbreaking work to try and fill a bushel basket with hard clams alone. It took about four hundred and fifty little necks, the smallest and most highly prized legal sized clams, to top off the rim. Still, it was enjoyable work often broken by passing marine wildlife like the big skate that once swam under my boat, wings protruding out from beneath both sides of the eight foot beam, or the seals that we sometimes saw sunning themselves on small islands during late February and early March. Sea turtles too, both Ridley's and leatherneck, were occasional visitors.

Perhaps what drew me to clamming the most was the chance to combine it with other activities like fishing. Always, a pole was left with the line in the water at the stern of the boat, a single clam or pair of piggyback snails draped from the hook a few inches above the sinker. Not a day ever passed when something didn't grab that bait and I enjoyed many a meal of fish fillet and cherrystone clam during those years. In the springtime, flounder and blowfish would be the day's bonus. Later in the season, sea trout, scup, summer flounder, small blues and, my favorite, the white-fleshed, succulent northern whiting (kingfish to us Yankees) would bite. It seemed as though no creature in the sea could pass up the tasty clam. Why then should we?

While I did much of my early clamming from above deck, it's a given that most recreational clammers actually gather their shellfish right alongshore or by wading shallow flats. That's fine with me, and since I no longer own a boat it's how I do it now. As before, though, I often combine my trips to the shore with other activities and so can you. Swimming, sailing, hiking, jogging, frisbee and, of course, fishing: all can be part of a clamming adventure. So can the down to earth luxury of a simple outdoor barbecue and a cold one.

But there's still much more to clamming than these practical and ordinary justifications. Clamming is really a frame of mind that allows you to recover and rebound from the pressures of an everyday world. There's a coastal flavor to this activity that many find as appetizing as the end result. Every time you stroll the beach your inner soul seems to reach out and grasp a little bit of nature, in the end allowing you to relax and feel more in touch with yourself. The more remote the setting the more intense the feeling. In between clamming trips, there's a yearning for more as each such excursion is a mini-vacation for the soul.

Textures, smells, sights and sounds: They all seem so refreshed at the seashore yet still so basic that their meanings are clear. The sea breeze carries gently a hundred different scents, each hinting at a new discovery just up ahead. Some days it's simply the smell of the sea that stands

There's a wide variety of interesting creatures and sights to see at the shore. Finding a lobster claw is not an uncommon thrill, though they rarely come so big as this one held by the author's daughter. On the opposite page, below . . .

out most. At other times it's the sweetly pungent fragrance of eelgrass scattered across the dampened foot of a sandy dune. It might even be the slightest whiff of menhaden or their relentless pursuers, the striped bass and bluefish, cruising close to shore. The true beauty of shellfishing lies in an understanding of its surrounding environment.

Stroll the edges of a muddy flat and you might observe a night heron tucked away in the crook of a small tidal creek. Intently the bird stares into the shallow water looking for the slightest movement ahead of its feet. Then suddenly, in a motion almost too quick to record, it picks a small shiner from among the bleached clam shells that litter the creek bed.

Out near the harbor mouth, common terns relentlessly work the rips, diving in a controlled sort of mayhem as they alternately scream and pluck migratory spearing or sand eels from the roiled waters. They never seem to miss. "Just how do they avoid colliding", you wonder? When you're sitting at the dock or back in your parked car they are just ordinary sea birds, little more than scoundrels actually, gliding back and forth with no particular justification for their existence except, perhaps, to drive fishermen crazy by snatching bags of baitfish from behind their backs. Grab your basket and step on the beach, however, and the terns take on beautiful colors, wonderful aerodynamic contours and a combination of speed and grace that few other seabirds can match. Suddenly, they are transformed into slick, competitive marvels.

Walk a little further across the flat and you might find a piece of driftwood, its rounded nubs smoothed by time and tide. Beside it may be an oyster "spike", a nearly foot long single shell bleached by years or even decades of relentless washing and sunshine. At one time it may have been harvested by a commercial bayman, perhaps the grandfather of someone you know. More likely, though, it died of old age. Pick it up and it feels smooth on one side, rough on the other, much like the personalities of many clammers that come to the flat.

. . . young girls examine a pair of tiny toads they've captured.

Fiddler crabs, too, may be encountered before you even reach for the first clam of the day. You'll see them scurrying to their burrows between the intertidal grasses as you approach. Have you ever stopped to examine the intricate tatoos on the backs of these tiny crustaceans? They sport several different colors, including handsome hues of red and purple. Corner a male and he will wave menacingly with his big claw. Easily he could be crushed by even a bare foot and he probably knows it, but in the past he has found this jesture enough to deter most humans and maybe a few small predators. Whether it is fear or compassion that removes the threat, he cares not.

Up ahead, there's a small tidal pool where the thieving tide has carved the sands from between a cluster of jetty rocks, creating the perfect seaside classroom for a youngster. At first glance, the waters of such a small puddle appear insignificant, just a little break from the otherwise well defined edging. Look closer, though, and it's teeming with all kinds of interesting life and their constant struggles to survive. A tiny zoo with countless inhabitants.

In the pool, a mix of grass and sand shrimp snap their way across the bottom while blue mussels and barnacles compete with the ever present slimy green algae to see which will cover the last remaining circle of bare granite. Snails of various species and sizes crawl across the stones, some above the water, some below. Pick one up to look inside and you might find it's not a snail at all but a stealthy hermit crab. A lesson in resourcefulness to be stored away in the mind of a child if someone takes the time to explain it.

In a shadow beneath a jagged, protruding edge, a quartet of young oysters are perched perpendicular to the bottom, shells slightly spread apart and cilia dancing rhythmically as water is siphoned in and out. Beyond the sun's reach, these four have found a place where they can eat both night and day while the other oysters and mussels choose to remain closed until the sun drops closer to the horizon. The feeding must be good, for this set is clearly the largest in the pool and the whole puddle seems to throb to their pulse, though it's really the tide which determines the beat.

Life may appear easy for the bivalves in this quiet water, but a closer inspection reveals some very real perils. Sitting atop a small rock just to the left to the oysters, a green crab feasts on the remains of a mussel he has somehow dislodged from its shell. Killifish, some as large as three or four inches, dart in and out of the small underwater crevices between the boulders, waiting for the crab to drop a tidbit from its perch. In the middle of the pool a great battle is being waged between another mussel and a rather large starfish. Though the action may seem slow or virtually non-existent to the casual observer, the hopelessly overmatched mussel is struggling for it's very life against what could be considered the king of tidal pool predators. With its suction cup covered arms grasping both sides of the mussel's shell, the starfish exerts tremendous pulling pressure as it attempts to tear open the bivalve. Fully tensed, it may continue pulling for ten or twelve hours if necessary, usually more than even the strongest shellfish can withstand. For now, things appear to be at a standoff, but eventually the starfish will prevail.

The tidal pool is but a single stop along the clammer's route. At the water's edge, or just below it, lies the driving force behind the trek.

Just shy of where the tide gently laps at the shore, a pair of six year-old boys race from fountain to fountain, delighted with the miniature geysers that some mysterious creature under the mud and gravel blasts knee high at the mere stamp of a foot. You walk by and smile at the

JOSEPH ALTMAN

parents, moving just a little further down the beach. The tide is perfect, exposing some of your favorite clam beds and the fact that so many steamers are spurting for the children is also encouraging. In no time at all, you know their juvenile curiosity will draw them to your small bucket for a peek. Perhaps they too will eventually be bitten by the clamming bug.

All this, and the real fun has yet to begin!

Two

Hardshell Clams

*A*h, to savor the salty sweet, delicate juices of a hardshell clam. Served raw on the halfshell, steamed, baked, fried or chowdered, this is the shellfish most familiar to American palates. It comes packaged naturally in a sturdy limestone container with just enough seawater to keep alive and fresh the tender contents that so perfectly complement a cold drink on a hot summer's evening. This is the shellfish which most wildly excites my taste buds, bringing the seashore to my lips even when I haven't the chance to be there in person. For those who pass it by on looks alone I sometimes feel a tinge of regret, for it is difficult to taste so succulent a seabreeze in any other creature.

Depending on where you live, this tasty delight may be called a round clam, bay clam or quahog (pronounced co-hog and spelled several different ways). Further, you may denote its size by tagging it a seed (too small to harvest), littleneck (minimum legal size to approximately two and one quarter inches across the shell at its widest point), cherrystone (two and a quarter inches to three inches across) or chowder clam (anything larger). As if that isn't enough to remember, Rhode Islander's alone reverse the meanings of littleneck and cherrystone, and New Yorkers choose to measure a clam by its thickness rather than width. Chowder clams are also referred to as "blunts", if smooth, old and worn looking, or "sharps" if they appear neat and well angled. In any case, because of its ability to maintain moisture for hours or even days by sealing itself shut inside that sturdy shell, the hard clam is easy to transport and store no matter its size or trade name; hence its vast commercial appeal.

Like most of the shellfish featured in this book, the hard clam is a bivalve member of the family *Mollusca*. (Bivalve means that it has two shells which can open and close.) It feeds upon plankton by straining water through a short, stout, double-tubed intake siphon which works much like a snorkel. As seawater is pumped into the siphon and past the gills by the constant motion of cilia, oxygen is transferred to the clam and food and minerals are extracted. It is also during this

American Indians made wampum out of hard clam and whelk shells. Aside from having religious meaning, it served as currency, jewelery and a sign of prestige.

process that the clam gains the lime salts needed to build its shell. Carbon dioxide and other waste materials are expelled as the water is flushed out the second tube. Because of the manner in which it feeds, hard clams grow best in areas with a light to moderate tidal flow or current.

Along with many of its shellfish relatives, the hard clam was first harvested in our waters by local Indians who used it to make a simple kind of currency called wampum. This early form of money, which to the Indian also held religious value, was nothing more than bead-sized pieces of clam and whelk shell strung together. The purple inside portion of the clam shell, called "Saki", was considered to have twice the value of the white fragments being that there was less of it to go around. While putting together a string of wampum must have been a taxing chore, I imagine it must have also been quite rewarding to walk down to the beach and truly *make* some money.

American Indians probably gathered their shellfish by sight or by probing the bottom with hands and feet, a method called "treading" which

Other types of shellfish, scallops and sea snails especially, are also used to make bracelets, necklaces and other types of human adornment.

is still popular today. Back then, our shores must have teemed with the tasty morsels, for the tribesmen left behind huge piles of empty shells. These piles or "shellfish middens" sometimes were enormous. Some measured over ten feet thick and covered as much as half an acre! Carbon dating has shown a few of the shells in these piles to date back as far as 4,000 B.C. The word "midden", by the way, simply means refuse heap.

Thick shelled and slow of foot (yes, the clam does have a muscle called a foot and it is used for locomotion), quahogs spend their lives underwater buried beneath the sand, mud or gravel. They remain primarily "subtidal" or below the low-water mark, which means that you'll have to get wet to dig them. Because they have a relatively short siphon, as compared to the long neck of a steamer, hard clams tend to lie only an inch or two below the sea floor. More adaptable to changing conditions and water salinity than are most other shellfish, they can live in bays, estuaries, shallow ocean areas, or even inside tidal rivers and creeks. Hard clams are generally found in what zoologists call *contagious distributions*. In layman's terms: where you find one you'll probably find a bunch more. They are especially fond of shallow "tidal flats", either sand or mud, and seem even more happy along the deep side edge of a sandbar. Studies show that their concentrations are most dense in a mixture of sand and shell substrate where water salinity levels range from 18 to 26 parts per thousand. Straight sea water averages about 35 parts per thousand.

Like many other kinds of shellfish, including oysters and steamer clams, the quahog usually begins its life as a male with about half the clams switching sex as they grow older. You can't tell the difference from an external examination, however, as males and females look identical. Both genders gear up for spawning in late spring and continue right on through mid-August with the males dispersing sperm and females expelling their eggs directly into the current. After the fertilized eggs hatch, the clam is in a larval stage, drifting free for two to four weeks before burying itself in the bottom for good. There it will blossom into an adult, adding growth rings to its shell much like those found in a log with the passing of each new summer. With a little luck, it will attain a harvestable size in three to five years. Quahogs can live to be 25 years old if left undisturbed by both predators and man.

Considering the simplicity of the creature, the number of harvesting methods devised to gather hard clams is rather surprising. They are caught with hands and feet, with modified pitchforks and specialized rakes, and, by some commercial fishermen, with hydraulic dredges that turn them up by the thousands per hour. They are taken from shore or boat, in water measuring less than a foot to depths of more than sixty feet.

While recreational shellfishermen usually locate oysters, mussels, whelks and scallops by sight, and at least have a clue as to the presence of softshell clams thanks to siphon holes, the lifestyle of the hard clam dictates that those who hunt it use an approach best described as "Blind Man's Bluff". Since the quahog spends all its time completely submerged underwater *and* underground, it leaves no visible indications of its presence. Thus, the only way to find them is to look for what appears to be suitable habitat, wade right in and give it your best shot.

Certainly, the least expensive method of clamming is to tread as the Indians and early American settlers did years ago. This task is quite easily accomplished in water up to about three feet deep, though it becomes increasingly difficult as you move out to greater depths. The term "treading" of course stems from the fact that this technique calls for the gatherer to actually step (tread) on the clams he finds. Essentially, the idea here is to shuffle flat-footed across the bottom, stopping to inspect anything that feels like a shellfish underfoot. Sounds easy enough, but there is definitely an art to this procedure and some people are far better at it than others. Still, with a little practice anyone can learn to tread enough clams for dinner. Since this methodology requires no more than a pair of shorts, sneakers and something to carry the captives in, it is probably the manner in which most people are introduced to hard clamming.

Generally speaking, prime treading bottom consists of soft sand or a semi-firm mix of sand and mud. Working in water clear and shallow enough to allow you to see the bottom is also a big plus. Once you've settled on a suitable location, begin prospecting by slowly walking along until you start to feel a few bumps underneath your feet. I like to start in knee-deep water and work deeper, but you could do the reverse. Either way, step gently and wiggle each foot into the sand to the point where the tops of your toes are even with the surface of the sea floor. As you dig in, your feet will come in contact with whatever treasures lie

Above: When treading, work your toes into the sand or mud to feel out hiding quahogs. Using a twisting motion helps.

Below: A group of treaders assume a classic clamming posture.

buried below. Any hard, round object that you happen to bump up against is likely to be a clam or a rock. Being able to tell the difference between the two is one of the talents that separates the expert from the novice. Since clams are able to anchor themselves firmly in place with their muscular foot, you will feel some resistance if you try to nudge them aside. The rocks, or other objects such as driftwood or old shells, will move with very little effort. It takes the beginner a while to learn how to equate this "stubbornness" to a clam — after all, clams of different sizes offer different levels of resistance — but with several successful trips under your belt it becomes second nature. Once you've determined that you have indeed stepped on (or up against) a clam, keep it pinned in place with your foot, then simply bend over and retrieve your prize by hand. In water that's over your waist, it might be necessary to bend over and dive since the body's inherent buoyancy makes it difficult to keep your balance when reaching deep. Although it isn't vital to success, treading is best done when the tide is low for then you can stray further from the shore and clam less frequently worked bottom.

While most neophytes hit the clam beds wearing nothing more than a pair of shorts and sneakers, experienced clammers like to go a few extra steps to ensure their safety and comfort. For instance, I like to do all my treading while wearing sweatpants and a long sleeve sweatshirt. This combats jellyfish and prevents the sun from baking me to the color of a steamed Maine lobster by the end of the day. (Sun blocks, by the way, aren't much help as they tend to wash off as soon as one enters the water.) If you know that you'll be clamming in shallow water, you might also consider wearing a tight fitting baseball style cap and, perhaps, a pair of polarized sunglasses.

It's hard to overstress the importance of wearing sneakers while you work. They are essential to safe treading. Over the years, I've seen quite a few treaders take their catch barefoot. In fact, some people prefer to simply lift clams from the bottom by grasping them with their toes. While this certainly requires less effort than bending over or diving, there's just too much risk of getting cut. In addition to keeping your toes covered, treaders should also wear a pair of gardener's gloves. This will alleviate the fear of slicing a finger while thrusting your hands deep into the sand or mud. I find that having the gloves gives me the security to really dig in and pry away at even the most stubborn quahogs.

Once you begin to achieve a modicum of treading success, you'll quickly find that having something to keep your catch in as you move about becomes a pressing concern. Most clammers either carry around a galvanized, metal bushel basket or pail that they can rest on the bottom when working in very shallow water, or tow a small inner tube with a bushel basket wedged tightly in the middle. The tire tube and basket is tied around the waist so that it follows wherever you go. Just be sure to leave six to ten feet of slack line so that you'll still be able to dive down and grab a clam when necessary.

Depending on how you see it, treading for clams is a lot of fun, tedious work, or both. What it isn't is the fastest way to gather clams. If you haven't the patience to catch quahogs one at a time, than maybe you would prefer to use a clam-rake of some sort, There are several kinds to choose from. These range from the simple claw style, to the rather genteel looking basket rake sold at tackle shops, hardware stores and tourist centers, to the sturdy bullrakes favored by professional clammers. For the raker, all the basics of treading apply as to locating clam beds, wearing proper clothing and footware, and having something to hold your catch.

The claw style rake allows you to scratch up clams two or three at a time. It really is little more than a modified garden rake and is used in a similar fashion, except its purpose is to remove clams rather than stones from an underwater garden. As the name implies, the head of this rake looks something like the claw of a bird of prey. The tines, or talons if you will, are spread about an inch apart and may number from three to twelve or so. Handle length varies but a six footer seems most comfortable in less than four feet of water.

The motion used to work a claw is akin to that used when raking garden rocks into a pile. Essentially, you begin by digging the tines into the bottom and with short, smooth strokes, try to pull the clams through the sediment and toward your feet. To do this efficiently, the rake's teeth must remain imbedded in the bottom at all times and the line worked should be straight as an arrow. Lifting the rake free will cause you to lose your place, and thus, your pile of quahogs. I like to work in a small, tight circle, standing in one place and rotating to my right with each new pass as I view the curious schools of snappers cruising by or watch the nesting gulls and red-wing blackbirds watching me from along a grassy marsh edge. To break the clams free of the bottom without losing them, fold the rake back away from your body until the handle sticks straight up like a flagpole. Lift the rake smoothly and your catch should remain balanced between the tines.

The basket rake is used in a similar fashion but it actually corrals the clams as you draw them toward you. Envision a carpenter's plane shaving down the edge of a door and you have an idea of how this rake works. The rake's teeth, usually three to four inches long and spaced an inch apart, serve as the blade by shaving clams off the bottom and deflecting them upward and into the trailing catch basket. Keeping the teeth at a proper angle to the bottom is the key. They must dig in and ride at about a 60 degree angle or else they'll simply slide over the shells. As with the claw rake, working straight lines in a circular pattern will allow you to thoroughly cover an area in good time.

As with treading, you'll quickly learn to tell the difference between a clam and a rock as it bumps against the tines. Again, the rocks move easily while the clams seem to resist. As long as you continue to feel some clams banging against the rake, keep right on digging without making a haul — that's why you have a basket behind the teeth. From time to time you're likely to stumble across a bed of densely packed clams. You'll know this because it will feel as though you are dragging your rake across a cobblestone road. It's then that you dig the hardest, making the most of such an opportunity. As you grow more experienced at raking, you'll also learn to tell by sound and feel

Basket rakes (foreground) and bullrakes are favored by most serious clammers.

when your basket contains old shells, bottles, or if you are lucky enough, even a scungilli. Sometimes you get a feeling that the rake is riding over the clams, scratching their tops as it goes past. If that's the case, stop and make sure there aren't any shells impaled on the teeth — they will keep the rake from digging in deep.

Claw and basket raking works especially well in conjunction with treading. Rather than waste your time and energy working bottom that may be devoid of clams, try finding the critters with your feet. When one is located, simply step back and rake it up. This will let you gather the clam you've found, plus any adjacent ones.

Ch-ching, ch-ching, ch-ching. There's no other sound quite like the rhythmic rattling of a bullrake full of hard clams being worked across the bottom by an expert shellfisherman. It's a sound pleasing to the ear, for it signals success in a blue collar endeavor yet foretells a white collar meal. If you are truly serious about hard clamming, you'll eventually buy and use one of these rakes.

Essentially, the bullrake is a commercial version of the basket rake. It is heavier, larger and more stout than the recreational tool and, depending on the model and style, capable of holding more than 100 clams in its rounded cage. In general, these rakes carry from 14 to 32 teeth spaced across the front of the head at one-half to one inch intervals. With the aid of flexible, telescoping aluminum poles they can be pulled by a clammer working from a drifting boat or wading like a basket raker. In either case, the poles and accompanying T-bar handle are set to equal a length which will allow the teeth to ride on the bottom at an appropriate angle. As with basket or claw raking, maintaining a good angle is the key to digging up a meal.

Bullrake teeth range from a length of one inch all the way up to awesome looking six-inch fangs. The shortest teeth are used strictly in sand, the largest in deep, soft mud. For the recreational clammer, a 16 to 24 tooth rake with two or three-inch tines will do just fine under most conditions. (Note: In some states, you need a commercial license to use one of these rakes and even then, special regulations may apply. In Delaware, for instance, it is unlawful for a recreational clammer to use any rake with a head larger than 14 inches across or a handle longer than seven feet.)

Simply put, bullraking, or "donkey raking" as it is often called, is the most productive way to gather quahogs with your feet in the water. Pulling one of these rakes it's possible to average eight or ten clams a haul. Sometimes, you'll do even better. While the technique parallels basket raking, there are a few small differences. For one thing, because these rakes feature a T-bar handle, you can really lean into the digging process. Once the teeth are firmly imbedded in the bottom, the bullraker rocks back and uses his weight to help work the tines underneath the clams. The pulling is accomplished in a series of short, rapid tugs designed to keep the teeth in the bottom while moving the rake ahead an inch or two at a time. Because bullrakes are rather heavy, you'll probably want to pace yourself carefully in this task. Thus, the standard rhythm calls for ten to twenty consecutive tugs, then a break of five or ten seconds. Another difference has to do with the time between hauls. While those who use basket rakes usually "pull up" whenever they feel a clam or two banging around inside the cage, the bullraker digs continuously for five or ten minutes before making a haul. Since the basket is so large, there is little fear of filling it up. By the way, whenever you lift your rake you should shake it vigorously back and forth just under the water's surface. This will clear away most of the mud and dirt, leaving you with shiny, clean clams to deposit in your basket.

Just how many clams can you catch in one haul of a bullrake? You'd be surprised. I remember my best effort coming in the early 1980's while working the beautiful sandy bottom of Great

The raker's routine: Dig in.   *Shake 'em clean.*   *Lift them over.*

South Bay off of Barrett Beach, Long Island. At the time I was about 20 years old and clamming commercially through the summer to help defray my college tuition. My goal for the day was to finish with a "count" of littlenecks, the commercial term for 500 of the smallest and most valuable legal-sized clams. Boy was I thrilled when the first lift of the morning revealed I had hit the jackpot — 104 glistening beauties. The sound of those clams tumbling across the iron bars as I emptied the rake into my wooden basket sounded *oh soooo sweet*. I distinctly remember thinking that it had a ring similar to coins pouring out of a slot machine at Atlantic City, which really was the case since a count of "necks" was then selling at about $80 and each clam in that haul was worth 16 cents.

Despite the occasional outstanding day, you should know that bullraking is tiring, back-breaking work. It will strain your muscles and blister your palms should you have soft hands (I find a pair of gloves helps with the blisters, nothing seems to help my back). The more you do it, however, the stronger you get and the easier it becomes. Just keep in mind that the larger the basket and bigger the teeth you use, the more effort it takes to pull the rake. When raking from

Pour them out.

Cull thoroughly.

And begin again.

Whether you rake on foot or from a boat, the important thing is to keep the teeth dug into the bottom. Leaning back helps increase leverage.

a boat, be sure to attach a small float — Clorox bottles work well — atop the rakehead with a 20- to 30-foot length of line. Then, should your rakehead ever accidently pull free of its pole, which does happen, it will be easy to locate and retrieve. A second float, secured to a sash weight of some kind, should also be at the ready to mark any hot clam beds you happen to rake across. This will allow you to return and drift over the exact same spot again and again.

A second kind of commercial clam rake sometimes used for recreational purposes, and always from an anchored boat, is the clam tong. These are good for use in water 3 to 18 feet deep. Clam tongs are constructed with a matched pair of wooden styles and work much in the same manner as a pair of kitchen tongs or hedge shears. As the clammer spreads the styles apart and then squeezes them shut above the water, opposing half-baskets at the business end of the rake separate and then mesh. Each basket side is armed by a set of tines measuring one-half to two and a quarter-inches long. As with the bullrake, the teeth are usually spaced at one-half to one-inch intervals. Since a pair of tongs can cost as much as $200 it is not the most common tool among "weekenders".

While most recreational clammers prefer to wade, there are some advantages to clamming from a boat that you should know about. To begin with, working from above the waves increases your range. Since not everyone can get out on the water, it stands to reason that deepwater clam-beds see less harvesting. Moving out over six to twelve foot depths that foot soldiers can never reach often helps improve the catch. Another boating plus is the extended season. Once the water turns cold in late October or early November, clamming on foot isn't much fun at all — not even in the diver's wet suits which some people

Tongers, often working in pairs, always dig from an anchored boat.

Laura Little Holt

like to use. Working from a boat, though, it's possible to clam year-round as long as the water remains unfrozen. Clamming from a boat also has its own set of unexpected thrills. Snagging a big fat flounder in your rake's teeth is not an uncommon spring or fall occurrence, and visits from seagulls or the tired butterflies which occasionally light on a wind-blown bow are certain to raise a smile or two. If you're lucky, you might even dig up a rakehead that someone else has lost, possibly still in good condition. I've found two so far.

No matter how you gather your clams, a gauge, ring or cull rack will be needed to help sort the legal sized ones from the seeds. A clam gauge is simply a small, flat, metal plate with a hole in the center. The hole is cut to match the minimum legal size for clams in the state where it is purchased. Any clam that fits through the hole is too small to keep and must be returned to the water unharmed. Clam rings follow the same logic, but instead of being rectangular like a gauge, they are circular. Some towns issue a free guage or ring when you purchase a clamming permit. Cull racks serve the same purpose as do gauges and rings, only these sort the clams a bunch at a time. They are constructed from a sturdy set of galvanized steel bars spaced at intervals equal to the minimum legal thickness for the clams in a particular state. Clammers simply pour their catch onto the rack at day's end and brush the clams back and forth with gloved hands while shaking the rack gently in an up and down manner. Any clam that drops completely through the bars is tossed back into the briny.

Three

STEAMER CLAMS

O f all the bivalves I've encountered over the years, these have been the most challenging and fun to catch. Ranging in color from bluish white or grey to a yellowish or bleached white, the steamer is surprisingly mobile. This is the "piss clam" or "squirter", the one which spurts a stream of water from below the mud or sand up to two feet in the air as it propels itself downward in an attempt to relocate or escape predation. It is delightful and fun to watch, and adults seem to get as much of a kick out of the geysers as do kids.

The name steamer probably originates from the popular practice of cooking this clam by steaming over seasoned water, beer or even white wine. In addition to the above tags, steamers go by several other nicknames. One is "softshell clam", the reason for which is obvious when you compare it side by side with the hardshell variety. Other nicknames such as "long neck" clam or "nannynose", reference its protruding, rubbery "neck" — actually a concealed pair of siphons used for feeding, breathing, breeding and waste disposal. Still another name I've heard the steamer called is

"Gaper". This tag fits especially well for when you
carefully examine a closed
steamer it never seems to be
sealed tight. There is, in fact,
almost always a small gap at
both ends. Because of this,
I've always found their appearance somewhat discon-
certing. And that neck . . .
ugh!

Somehow, though, after
you've looked at a few dozen steamers their appearance begins to grow on you. They become a
familiar and welcomed sight. And, you must
admit, their peculiar shape does serve them well
for it allows them to easily slice through sand, mud
or even gravelly substrate to surface at feeding
time and retreat when threatened.

The steamer's range is vast, covering Arctic
waters to as far south as the Carolinas. Fortunately for us, they seem to be most plentiful inshore,
especially along the New England, New York and
Chesapeake coastlines. Here they burrow into
mud flats and sandbars leaving nothing more than
a small "squirt hole" to denote their presence. It is
these quarter-inch wide holes, as you'll see, that
are the key to deciding just where to try and dig
these creatures.

Over the years, softshells have kind of been like
Avis Rent-A-Cars: they're "the other clam". While
hard clams have always had a place in the retail
market, steamers have been used for such in-
glorious purposes as fertilizing fields and, as bad,
fattening livestock. In fact, during the early

1900's, prize winning pigs in many areas were slopped with a mix of steamers and corn. Today, though, this delicious mollusk is fast attaining favor as a plentiful and inexpensive treat. I only hope that its populations can support the added pressure over the next few decades. The concern isn't so much about overharvesting or lack of fecundity as it is for habitat destruction and water pollution. The restrictive intertidal zone in which these shellfish grow is so very fragile and too often encroached upon by man.

In general, steamers thrive on shallow flats which come to be fully exposed twice a day at low tide. It's therefore essential that you check the tide tables ahead of time. Were it not for the water leaving the premises as the tide bottoms out, these are the same kinds of areas you might think suitable for hard clams. In fact, many steamer hot spots lie adjacent to quahog beds, making it easy to gather a basket full of each if you know how. The steamers, though, do show a preference for a little extra salinity.

As do most bivalves, steamers live in large groups called "colonies" and on choice feeding grounds more than two dozen may crowd together in a single square foot of bottom. They seem especially fond of clean mud flats, probably because these offer high nutrient content (aka: clam food!) from decaying aquatic eelgrass and other plant and animal life. If there is enough microscopic fodder in the water, steamers are also quite capable of living in sandy or rocky areas. Being filter feeders, they need a moderate current or tidal flow to survive. They do not readily establish themselves in inlets or swift moving channels and, being somewhat brittle, can't survive a pounding surf. Stagnant waters will prove barren, too.

Adult steamers run from about an inch to three and a half inches across the shell, though some may reach a length of more than six inches. When left undisturbed, they'll position themselves vertically at a depth which allows the siphon to reach slightly above the bottom. This is usually from two to five inches deep. A few will undoubtedly go deeper as the siphons of some steamers have been measured at up to 15 inches. As the tide recedes, the neck is retracted and the clam burrows down an additional inch or two to escape a bright sun or add a buffer zone between itself and potential predators.

At the end of the shell opposite from the siphon is the steamer's "foot". This hard muscle is used to anchor the clam in place while feeding and is its primary means of locomotion. While the squirt produced by the contraction of a steamer neck may help propel the clam through the sand, it is the foot that leads the way, contracting and expanding, pushing and pulling to break apart the sediment which otherwise would be impenetrable.

In the most southerly reaches of their domain, steamers spawn almost continuously during June and July, and intermittently through September. From Massachusetts north, they may not begin the love process until mid-July when the waters have sufficiently warmed. As with hard clams, mating is unromantic; the spermatazoa and eggs are jetisoned out the siphon of males and females respectively, then mixed by the sea. If one percent of the fertilized eggs survive, the spawning season has been a big success. In their larval stage, the

Typically, steamers come from soft-bottomed sand or mud flats. Healthy colonies exhibit an even mix of sizes, as shown at right. Because you'll be poking or digging through the sediment, a pair of gloves is a necessity — even if you plan on using a rake or pitchfork.

young clams will spend about five days floating or swimming before settling to the bottom. Already they show a tendency towards restlessness and spend a week or two inching across the bottom with the aid of byssus threads (thin, rough, protein fibers like those found on a mussel) until finally deciding on a more permanent home. At the time of its "set" (the point at which a shellfish decides to basically stay put) the steamer measures about one sixteenth of an inch long. In two to three summers, depending on climate and food supply, it will be big enough to harvest.

Whereas treading, raking and tonging hard clams is done blind with little more than a "feeling" that the critters are underfoot, those who gather steamers actually pinpoint their prize by sight. The tip-off comes in the form of those little squirt holes these fellows leave behind as they burrow about and expel water from their siphons. Simply put, wherever you find steamer holes, you'll find steamers. Obviously, then, you'll want to do your digging where you find the *most* squirt holes.

Because you have to spot 'em before you start to dig 'em, the most important thing to keep in mind when gathering softshell clams is to work while the tide lays low. This point just can't be overstressed for it is the key, the crux, the vital factor to accessing steamer colonies. Show up when the water covers the flats and you'll never see a single steamer hole, much less a dimple. Get the picture?

How far down must the water draw before the games begin? That depends on the area you intend to work. At some locations, productive beds are high and dry by the time the tide drops to the halfway point. In other areas, only the last two hours of outgoing will leave the flats exposed. You really need to do some homework to be sure. In fact, it's not a bad idea to keep a record of the best time to clam your different hotspots, just to keep from getting confused. It sounds too simple to mess up, but you'd be amazed how easy it is to miss the tide at some locations, even for a so-called expert.

One time I invited my publisher and his friend down for a little steamer hunting on Long Island. At the chosen location I had taken both steamers and hard clams on several prior occasions, but always at dead low tide. Imagine my red face when we arrived but two hours into a rising tide and found the beds already covered by four to six inches of water. Since I had never before worked the area on a rising tide, I had no way of knowing how fast those mudflats could disappear. Because of that experience, when I take someone along

Working the mudflats for steamers can result in some rather interesting discoveries like the find above, a steamer that grew to adult size inside a small medicine bottle. At left, a young clammer hoists the top half of a giant tape worm; the bottom half lays coiled in the lower left corner of the picture.

these days I make sure I arrive at least two hours *before* dead low tide. That way, there can be no missing the action. By the way, you can find "tide charts" in most local newspapers and a few local fishing magazines. These usually provide a one week schedule of high and low tides.

One last thought on tides before we move on: Make it a point to plan a trip each year around the perigee tides. This is the point at which the moon is the closest to the earth and, as such, exerts its strongest tidal influence. At this time the tide rises

For the steamer gatherer, it's vital to be on the grounds for the lowest stages of the tide. In some locations, you'll only have an hour or two each day when the flats are fully exposed.

to its highest point of the year, and more importantly, drops to its lowest level. This all boils down to clam beds being exposed that may not be accessible at any other time of the year. It should go without saying that the low side of the new and full moon "spring" tides, which occur each month, are also prime time for steamer digging.

Since steamers live in mud, sand or rocky soil, you have to work to get them out, and it can't be done without getting dirty. Because of this, you can start preparing for your day at the shore by selecting old clothes. I like to wear a pair of old sneakers (forget about socks), denim jeans or shorts and a T- shirt. Instead of sneakers, most professional and some well prepared recreational gatherers use knee high or hip boots. These would probably be a good investment if you plan on taking more than a few trips for steamers each year as they will keep you cleaner and drier while you work. I like the denim pants because they are perfect for wiping dirt off your hands as you go about your business. They seem coarse enough to brush off the grit, yet keep much of the mud from

reaching the covered portions of your skin. They are, of course, also comfortable.

One definite requirement when digging for steamers is a pair of quality gardening gloves. These are necessary because you will be picking through, digging in and scooping up mud, sand and gravel without much time to look for sharp or protruding objects like cracked shells, broken glass, jagged rocks and pieces of wood or other debris. If you think it's important to protect your feet when clamming, just imagine what a risk it would be to work with an uncovered hand.

Now we come to the meat of the matter, how to actually dig some steamers — and the operative word here is *"dig"* for that's just what one does when gathering this shellfish. There are several ways of going about this task, though the basic technique is the same for all but one. Let's start with the method that requires the least in the way of tools: using just your hands.

Assuming you've got a beat on some steamer holes, approach quietly and avoid stepping directly on them. Heavy feet are a sure means of alarming the clams and sending them burrowing deeper. You want to keep them near the surface so they'll be easier to grab as you start digging.

Get into a kneeling position beside the holes and prepare for battle. With your gloved hands cupped together, quickly scoop up as big a chunk of soil as you can. Deposit your pile to the side and immediately reach for a second, third and fourth load until the hole in front of you is about a foot in diameter and six to twelve inches deep. If there are any clams at the base of the hole or along its sides, grab them now. This first assault must be a blitzkrieg, for it will immediately send adjacent softshells diving deeper, making them infinitely harder to pry out.

By this point, you've probably spotted a clam or two in the displaced soil. Pick them out and place them aside or in your bucket. Now run your fingers back though the pile, breaking apart the sediment and feeling for any clams you might have missed. You can now turn your attention back to the hole. In it, you might find a tunnel where a clam sliced off to the side since they move horizontally as well as vertically through the sediment. If so, scoop out that part of the hole some more — usually the clam is only an inch or two out of sight. If not, begin widening the hole in a general manner by scooping from the bottom and along the base of the walls. Digging out the bottom will cave in the top, constantly increasing the width of the hole and rolling new clams into the middle of the basin which by now should be shaped like a big Chinese wok. Keep scooping out the sediment and culling through it for clams. By the time the hole has reached two to three feet across, it's time to move on to the next ambush area. Before you do, however, make it a point to push back the soil you've removed. You should also replant any baby clams you may have uncovered.

I like to work about an arm's length from the tidal line with my back to the water while I'm digging this way. This allows me to make a tiny channel from the water to my excavation sight. If you build a small soil dam, you can open it up every few scoops to allow a little water to flow into your basin. This will flush and break apart the sediment, helping you to dig more quickly. It's kind of like clamming and building a sand castle at the same time, something big kids like me find entertaining.

While gathering clams with your hands alone may be sporty, it's not the the most productive way to fill a basket. It just seems to be a little too slow and a tad too dirty for most of us. Therefore, advanced clammers generally use some type of tool

Digging steamers with just your hands can be pretty challenging sport. Not only can they move quickly through the sediment, they may also scoot off in any direction, even horizontally (see inset). Be sure to replant the seed clams that are too small to harvest by dropping each, siphon up, in a finger-sized hole poked in the bottom.

when they dig. Nothing fancy here, just something to help get the job done.

Believe it or not, one of my favorite digging aids is a pair of long, wooden salad spoons. With wide, slightly curved ends and long handles, these are perfectly designed tools for scooping up loose, wet soil. With them, I can even single out a specific steamer by quickly inserting one spoon deep behind a squirt hole and literally popping the clam out of the ground along with a spoonful of sediment. Mostly, though, I use the spoons to help widen the holes I've started with my hands. They improve my efficiency by lifting more dirt per scoop. They also penetrate better than a hand when digging in hard ground. If you don't like the idea of using spoons, you can substitute a garden spade. These dig even better than the spoons, but tend to crack a lot of clams in the process, leading to a fair amount of waste. Too much waste, I think.

For years and years, serious steamer gatherers have relied on pitchforks to help them collect dinner and there can be no denying that the use of this farm implement can produce a bucketful of clams in a hurry. With this approach one simply digs in along the edge of a steamer colony and turns over a load of sediment. The fork lifts enough in one shot that most of the clams are busted free. The steamers are then picked from the overturned pile. Some clammers like to work a forkful at a time, others will turn over five or six chunks of soil then go back and cull through each one. As with digging by hand, you'll want to break apart each forkful of sand or dirt to make sure you don't miss any clams. You'll also want to fill the holes back in and replant any "seed" you've uprooted.

Though the use of pitchforks is a little less trying on the back than digging by hand, I have a problem with this method of taking shellfish and apparently so do a few other people. Because the pitchfork is so powerful and rigid, it crushes, spears, smashes, splits and cracks a disproportionate number of clams. This might not be so noticeable in areas where the steamers are spread apart, but in densely populated beds it seems that almost every forkful taken mangles a clam or two. I'm also sure the pointed forks destroy other kinds of marine life such as seaworms. In fact, I no longer use a pitchfork (or even a spade) when I clam. I just can't justify the waste. A few people use regular garden rakes and these seem to do a little less damage being that they only scalp those clams in the top two or three inches of soil. Still, it doesn't seem worth the cost. If you clam in rocky areas — I don't, usually — you may find pitchforks, shovels and rakes to be the only practical way of turning over soil fast enough to catch a few clams. Presently, several states are considering outlawing the use of shovels, pitchforks and the likes on steamer grounds, arguing that they destroy too many clams, sea worms, crabs, etc. It sounds like a good idea to me.

Recently, a new clamming device has hit the market and it has the potential to change forever the way we gather steamers. It's called "The Clam Catcher".

Constructed of high impact PVC tubing, the clam catcher weighs but seven and a half pounds. Using nothing more than air suction for power, it can travel down through two feet of wet sand or mud in only two seconds. You simply place the base of the 3-inch wide barrel over a steamer hole, create suction by pulling up on the plunger while pushing down on the main handle, and lift a clean, perfectly cylindrical column of sediment from the flat. Trapped inside the bottom of the unit is whatever was down there to begin with. Push down on the plunger and the column falls to the ground with your clam intact and undamaged. The premise is so simple you'll wonder why no one thought of it sooner.

This invention appears to be almost unbreakable in the field and best of all, it doesn't harm the environment. Even sand, tape and blood worms come up whole and unbroken, and quahogs and razor clams can be lifted too, provided they live in the intertidal zone. The Clam Catcher, which also comes in a two-inch barrel size for extracting salt water baits such as grass shrimp, fiddler crabs and sand fleas, has already been approved for use by the Environmental Protection Agency and shellfish bureaus of many coastal states. With some states currently thinking about eliminating rakes, etc. as stated above, it's possible that in some areas this unit may soon be the only tool one can use to dig steamers. If you would like to find out more about it, you can write to the inventor himself, Mikie B. Catcher, at Mikie's Bait Catcher, 1515 Weaver Street, Scarsdale, NY 10583.

The Clam Catcher is a unique device which literally sucks steamers, razor clams and quahogs from their intertidal beds. Aside from being very effective, it's much less environmentally destructive than a clam rake or pitch fork — and it dosen't break any clams.

Wherever and however you gather steamers, make it a point to skip around a little as you dig. Take a few in one spot, then move several feet away before lifting some more. This will prevent you from "cleaning out" any particular colony. It will also increase your catch in the long run since the clams will all be digging in deep around the last area worked. Moving around lets you sneak up on a whole new set.

The prehistoric looking horseshoe crab is a frequent visitor to the tidal flats which steamers love. Here a baby horseshoe, only a little larger than the cherrystone shell in the background, makes its way across a shallow pool. Note the pair of big steamer holes in the foreground.

Four
OYSTERS, MUSSELS AND SCALLOPS

*I*f quahogs and steamers are the meat and potatoes of the shellfisherman's catch, then oysters, mussels and scallops must be the *piece de resistance*. They provide the contrast needed to prime one's taste buds, to pique culinary curiosity and broaden our fun at the shore. They are, in fact, more endearing than the clam to many for they seem to present a more intimate persona. Perhaps this reflects their less widespread availability, or maybe, its due more to their worldly appearence: none of the three would ever consider hiding anonymously beneath the sand.

Stroll along a marshy shore and you might spot a solitary oyster, or perhaps several, rising up from the muddy edge of a back harbor shoreline, cove, creek bed or lagoon. From afar, they almost look like beckoning hands inviting you over for closer inspection. Nearer to the ocean, along jetties, bulkheads and rocky shores, armies of mussels stand proudly at attention. The Queen's Guard of shellfish, they seem completely absorbed in duty. Then there is the magnificent scallop: an underwater flamenco dancer flaunting its skirted beauty for all the world to view. Pick one up, place it in your bucket and watch as it performs especially for you, opening and closing with a happy castanet-like sound that defies captivity. Truth be known, the scallop is a tease. Still, were any of these shellfish species people, you'd surely cross the street to shake hands and say hello — a simple nod of recognition would never do.

Appearances aside, oysters, mussels and scallops are more easily gathered than you might think. Though you may have to look hard to find them along some parts of the coast the rewards are worth the effort. Enjoy them whenever you can for if variety is truly the spice of life, this fine trio may very well be the anise, basil and Rosemary of shellfishing.

THE AMERICAN OYSTER

There's no mistaking our American breed of oyster for any other shellfish. It's unique in shape and flavor and permanently secured to its perch. Though sometimes called the Eastern oyster, it has also been introduced along the gulf and west coasts. One of the oldest species of marine life known to man, it has changed relatively little over the past 200 million years.

Like snowflakes, no two oysters are exactly alike. Though the chalky, rough-edged shells may resemble each other to some degree, each is uniquely contoured. As a flowering plant stretches for sunshine, the oyster shapes its shell in an attempt to maximize living space and better reach protein-rich waters. If competition from other oysters is keen, the shells grow long and thin. Less pressured oysters are often short and wide, almost

Oysters grow to utilize available space and no two are shaped exactly alike. While some are round and others long and thin, they are all the same species. If left undisturbed to grow, oysters can get quite large, sometimes reaching 14 inches in length.

round. Most fall somewhere in between.

The key to locating oysters lies in finding a source of nearby unpolluted freshwater, for this species is estuarine in nature. Although it can survive in the open ocean it will not spawn in salty seas. Hence, oysters frequent tidal creeks or often the backside stretches of bays and harbors. Shallow flats aligning with small freshwater springs that drain through thick marsh are a favored setting. In northern waters where they may be threatened by prolonged periods of sub-freezing temperatures, oysters generally choose to live below the tide line, growing in scattered colonies or "clusters" of up to a hundred individuals. In more southern climes they mostly grow intertidally with the clusters being called "hands".

You've no doubt heard at one time or another that oysters shouldn't be taken in those months spelled without an "R", July for example. While many mistakenly believe that sickness will result from violation of this shibboleth, the saying actually stems from early attempts at oyster conservation. Lawmakers noted as early as 1770 that oysters spawn in those months lacking the scarlet letter. Thus, the prohibition on summertime gathering.

As with most other bivalves, some oysters change from male to female as they age and it's virtually impossible to tell the difference between the sexes without an autopsy. One thing is certain, however: oysters try very hard to be prolific. Scientific estimates vary widely as to the number of eggs a female can produce with guesses ranging from 60 million to more than 500 million.

As with clams, oysters release their eggs and sperm directly into the water. Within about 24 hours of fertilization, free swimming larvae develop and begin propelling themselves by the controlled pulsing of cilia. After one to three weeks, the larvae drift to the bottom where they must quickly locate a hard surface for permanent attachment — those that fail perish. The survivors quickly secrete a fluid cement to bond their bottom shell forever in place. From that point on, this shell will grow relatively flat and straight while the top shell becomes more convex and rounded. While almost any clean, hard surface is acceptable for attachment, old oyster shells appear to be the ultimate spat conductor. Once the selection of a residence is decided upon and the bond complete, a "set" is said to have occurred. The juveniles or "spat" will then need four to five years to attain a harvestable size of three to five inches. If left alone to grow, oysters may live 10 years or more and reach a length of 15 inches.

Of course, no discussion of oysters would be complete without touching on the subject of pearls. These are nothing more than small, gritty or sandy irritants to the oyster which for some reason it cannot eject. To ease its discomfort, the oyster coats the offending particles with the same slick, "Mother of Pearl" material it uses to decorate the inside of its shell. The resulting round bead may have a market value reaching into the thousands of dollars depending on its lustre, color, size and shape. Your chances of finding a natural pearl in any American oyster, however, are about 1 in 1,000.

While oysters can be harvested by boaters using special tongs or rakes, it's not likely that many recreational gatherers will go this route. Thus, I'll stick here to a discussion of taking them in a more leisurely fashion. For most of us, a basket and big flathead screwdriver will be the only necessary adjuncts.

Oyster gathering is straightforward: you try to pry them free and they stubbornly resist. The first move is to simply grab an oyster in a gloved hand and give it a twist or shake to see if it might come loose. Failing in this, the gatherer next inserts the flat head of a screwdriver or similar straight edge as deep as possible between the oyster and its anchor. Using the opposite hand, a foot or even a knee to hold the creature in place and create leverage, pry the oyster loose and place it in a sack or pail. It's that simple. Usually, the gatherer wins, but there are some specimens so solidly attached to large rocks or immovable objects that they are almost impossible to break loose. Those guys usually get to stay behind.

To what an oyster can adhere will sometimes amaze you. Although their availability is greatly restricted by habitat requirements, they are fairly adaptable within the proper niche. For example, just this summer I took a 13-inch-long oyster that had attached itself to a small stone little more than the size of a half dollar. It was standing all alone on a quiet sandbar. On another occasion, I found

Usually, oysters attach themselves to large, sturdy objects. Sometimes, though, they will adhere to smaller items and appear to sprout right out of the bottom. Those growing intertidally, like the ones shown at left, are referred to as "meadow oysters".

them sprouting from a barge planted along a tidal creek to prevent erosion. To this day I doubt that anyone else has discovered this bed as it's hidden beneath a ledge and the shellfish aren't visible unless you hang over the side, tuck your head under the lip and look up (Don't ask why I did this). After a windy fall storm, you might also find small clusters of oysters lying in the shallows, having been uprooted anchor and all and rolled toward the beach by wind driven waves. Keep your eyes peeled for these whenever you walk the shoreline after a good blow and you might be pleasantly surprised.

Although there is some degree of flavor variation, most oysters have a delicate, almost buttery taste and a scent that distinctly hints of "sweet water" environs. Still the glamor boy of shellfish, they maintain a dedicated following. True oyster aficianados can be so discerning as to actually differentiate by taste the locations from which various oysters originate. The most famous strain, the Blue Point oyster, was said to be the "smoothest" and "sweetest" tasting of them all. While the name still exists, the Blue Point is now grown and gathered within the confines of Long Island Sound and though still very good, I've been told that a "special something" was lost when the last of the natural harvest failed in Great South Bay sometime around 1950. Today, the most popular strain is probably the Chincoteague, well known for its salty flavor. There are, of course, many other strains found along our shores, enough to keep even the most passionate oyster lover guessing as to where the one he is eating came from.

BLUE MUSSELS

While the chances of finding a pearl in an oyster are pretty slim, the odds of finding one in a blue mussel must run one in several dozen. Sometimes you'll find two or three at once as you accidentally crunch them while chewing a piece of mussel meat. Now before you run out the door looking to make a fortune, let me assure you that the tiny "Mother of Pearl" deposits sometimes found in this bivalve are usually unsymmetrical and commercially worthless, though the elongated freshwater pearls now so common on earrings actually come from a species of cultivated freshwater mussel.

The blue mussel is well named, for it possesses a beautiful, blackish-blue hue. Measuring three to five inches long when mature, this smooth-shelled mollusk adheres to virtually any hard object including bridge abutments, jetties, rocks, boulders, bulkheads, unprotected boat bottoms, other mussels, oysters and even driftwood. Once, I even found a small colony attached to a rock that was wedged inside a discarded sneaker!

Never let it be said that the mussel doesn't like company for it thrives in tight clusters numbering from a couple to more than a thousand. In areas where suitable habitat is widely available, such as along a jetty or breakwall, you may chance upon tens of thousands. With the tide drawn down and the beds exposed, you might even smell 'em before you spot 'em! Large colonies have a distinct scent that I can only describe as being similar to a wet anchor line. Only a trained nose would notice, as the smell is quite neutral and unoffensive.

While blue mussels usually grow in tight, interwoven clusters that are fully exposed, bank mussels grow as unattached individuals half buried among intertidal grasses. The bank mussel can also be easily identified by its brownish, ribbed shells.

Generally speaking, mussels prefer to habitate intertidal zones close to open water. That's because they require large amounts of fresh sea water and oxygen to survive. Scientists estimate that each of these filter feeders strains about 12 gallons of water an hour. Multiply that by 24 hours and several thousand individuals and you can begin to understand why they are never found in stagnant areas. Like oysters and clams, microscopic plankton are the staple of their diet.

Because of its great abundance, choice of habitat, smooth contour and inability to scoot away, the mussel is the easiest of shellfish to gather. Just walk over to where you see them and start picking. In fact, so simple is this shellfish to catch that some clammers have to remind themselves not to take too many. Most accessible mussel beds are found slightly above the low water mark but these shellfish also thrive beneath the surface, as any marine scuba diver will attest.

There are really two common types of edible mussels to be found in local waters. The second kind is the ribbed or bank mussel. While also

Blue mussels adhere to almost any hard surface but are especially fond of rocks and concrete. Here, the author gathers a handful of tasty treats from classic mussel habitat. Bridge abutments and rock jetties offer the opportunity to pick mussels that reside well above the bottom. This often results in superior flavor and less grit inside the shell.

edible, this impostor is not quite so appetizing or numerous as the blue. Aside from taste, it is differentiated by its ribbed or grooved shell and dirty brown tint. Additionally, while the blue mussel is always found growing in clusters above the ground, the ribbed version grows as separate individuals half buried among the intertidal grasses. Their appearance sometimes reminds me of the old "pop up" toys Buster Brown Shoe stores used to give out to children, for they come in tightly packed sets but each is clearly a separate individual. As a general rule, blue mussels make their way to the dinner plate, ribbed mussels to the fisherman's chum pot.

While the blue mussel is not as mobile as a clam, it is less stationary than an oyster. If conditions mandate, they can move a few inches over the course of the year. The key to mussel locomotion lies in the byssus threads (those frizzy beards) which they use to anchor themselves in place. To relocate, the mussel secretes a jelly-like substance which hardens into the stringy byssus soon after contacting sea water. With expert aim, the jell is shot at an object in the desired direction of travel. After the byssus hardens, some of the old strings are released and the mussel tilts ever so slightly toward its ultimate goal. The process is repeated time and again until the shellfish is fully satisfied with its new location.

The term "picking" truly comes to mind when gathering this shellfish for, in most cases, mussels are simply plucked from their perch. No special tools are required and the technique is easy to master. Select the mussel of your choice and grasp it firmly in a gloved hand with your thumb and forefinger on opposite sides of the hinge and as close as possible to the point of attachment. Now, with a twist of the wrist, pop it free. The methodology is not unlike pulling an apple or a pear from a tree, though here you'll have to reach down rather than up. Talk as you work, yell, shout, scream if you like, jump up and down: the mussels aren't going anywhere. Unlike steamer clams, these troopers stay put while you harvest them. Because their byssus beards frequently intertwine, it's often possible to grasp and pull free entire clusters of mussels at once, dropping them in your bucket or bag a handful at a time as though they were a big bunch of purple grapes.

The sturdy appearance of the mussel in its shining blue armor and massive regiments belies its fragility. They are not hard shelled like oysters or quahogs. They crack or break when handled roughly and crush easily when trod upon. With this in mind, I've not discussed taking them with pitchforks, rakes or tongs. I prefer, instead, to encourage you to work by hand, carefully picking along the perimeter of the beds. This will prevent excessive destruction of these delicate shellfish and ensure that the heart of the colony remains intact.

Mussels are the ideal shellfish for children to gather. They can be caught without wading in deep water, require no tools other than a pair of gloves and their vast numbers virtually guarantee success. Also, they are frequently found within sight of sandy beaches suitable for swimming. With a little planning, the entire family can enjoy some fun in the sun both before and after filling their baskets.

BAY SCALLOPS

If only these were more plentiful, I think they would be the hands-down favorite of most shellfishermen.

With its fancy designer jacket and mobility that leaves other mollusks in the dust, the scallop appears to be vastly different from the other shellfish we've discussed. To a large degree, it is. Whereas clams, mussels and oysters each utilize matched pairs of adductor muscles to open and close their shells, the scallop relies on a single large one. What's more, most Americans pass up the adductors on other shellfish but specifically seek out this muscle on the scallop, discarding the body. Europeans eat the  whole thing. Further separating this shellfish from the ranks of ordinary bivalve mollusks is the scallop's claim to a patron saint. The apostle Saint James wore a scallop as his personal emblem, hence the name "Coquille Saint Jacques" (Saint James's shell).

Then too, there is the mobility factor. By rapidly opening and closing their shells, scallops can spurt jet streams of water from their wide end and quickly dart ahead several feet at a time. Sometimes, they'll glide a foot or more off the bottom in full flight, then toggle back down like a quarter dropped into a deep pool.

Scallops also possess a set of primitive blue eyes capable of sensing changes in light. Thus, they will occasionally scoot away when crossed by a dark shadow, although this happens much less frequently than some might have you believe.

Several kinds of scallops inhabit American waters. One confusion causer that quickly comes to mind is the sea scallop — flat in appearance, finely ribbed and sometimes measuring eight inches across its shell. Though live specimens are rarely found by the recreational gatherer, the big shells do occasionally wash up on shore, leaving the finder to wonder where a scallop so large might be found nearby. The reality is that this creature is a deepwater dweller, most often dredged commercially from offshore ocean beds lying fifty miles or more from the nearest beach. The calico scallop, on the other hand, is a recent European import generally mottled brown or reddish in color and almost always measuring less than two and a half inches across the shell. It has established itself along the southern and Gulf coasts over the last thirty years or so. Both sea and calico scallops are edible. That said, it is the "Bay" or "Cape" scallop which interests us here.

As the name implies, the bay scallop is most fond of protected, shallow inshore flats. Its love of exceptionally clean, shallow water makes it quite accessible to the recreational gatherer who knows of such a spot. Mind you, this shellfish spawns during the summer months and, in the name of conservation, seasons for taking it are mostly scheduled for the fall, winter and spring. For that reason, "capers" are usually caught while wearing a pair of waders. As the season grows late, jackets and hooded sweatshirts also become standard garb.

Although bay scallops are fast growers by

shellfish standards, they live only 1 1/2 to 2 years and spawn but once. During the spawn, virtually all their energy is devoted to reproduction and even shell growth temporarily ceases. When the spawn ends and normal shell growth resumes, a well defined ring is left behind to decorate the scallop's outer shell edge, denoting where growth had stopped. That's convenient for gatherers as this ring can be used to determine if a scallop is big enough to harvest. Those without the ring haven't yet had a chance to procreate and should, naturally, be returned. Mature scallops usually measure two and a half to three and a half inches across the shell at its widest point.

Since a good drive may be required to find a bay or harbor you'll have to more or less make a commitment to head out with scallops, not just shellfish, in mind. More importantly, you need to be in the mood for scalloping. That isn't hard, though, once you've tasted the rewards of such effort.

As tiny killifish and scattered pods of spearing weave between waving strands of eelgrass, the scalloper quietly stalks along. The most casual gatherers will be found working parallel to the inshore edge of the beds, probably in knee deep water. Pick one out and watch him carefully. You'll see that every few steps he stoops over to grasp a scallop in his gloved hand. Each captive is checked to make sure the tell-tale ring is present. Immature "bugs" are released while "keepers" are carefully placed in a basket, pail, or bushel bag tied to a belt loop. With each yard of advance, the scalloper is treated to a slight change in underwater scenery. To the left, a sand crab withdraws to safer depths, scurrying past a line of moss green stones. Over on the right and up ahead a bit, a starfish looks content relaxing between two empty sets of ridged shells. Peering hard at the bottom, as if trying to read the fine print on an eye chart, the gatherer wishes he had lifted the polaroid sun glasses from the dashboard before setting out. He bends slowly forward; "Is that one between the rocks live or dead?" he wonders. Turning his head to the side as his shirt sleeve dips below the cool surface, he retrieves an empty shell. Perhaps it now occurs to him that he's retracing the starfish's route. Just as easily, though, the next scallop could be alive.

A more serious scalloper might use a viewer and small, round scoop net. This is a great way to get intimate with the bay bottom. Basically, a viewer is a big wooden or plastic box with the bottom cut out and a piece of Plexiglas inserted in its place. A plastic milk crate is the usual choice but anything along that line will do so long as it floats — or can be made to.

With the transparent bottom of the viewer riding flat against the surface, you can clearly see underwater if you stick your head over the box and use your body to block out most of the sun. Move along slowly and the sea floor reveals its treasures as though you were wearing a diver's mask. Look carefully, and you'll scope your first scallop, shells partly opened as it strains plankton from the current. Notice how it looks like it belongs right where it sits. Left undisturbed, nature rarely misplaces its jewels. A scoop of the net and the prize is yours.

Continue on and other creatures soon begin to

Using a viewer and round scoop net is a great way to tour the bottom and gather up some tasty delights. It reminds one of crabbing, though it's not quite as sporty.

reveal themselves. A frequent friend is the baby winter flounder. Remarkably camouflaged to match the bottom, it's rarely ever noticed. The discerning eye might also spot a stray blowfish, blueclaw crab or whelk. Look up now and scan the shoreline; the leaves are in full turn and a tight flock of sandpipers flying by sparkles against dark blue waters to your east. Moving off, they look like diamonds in the sky, silvery reflections of sunbeam bouncing off their wings in every direction as they parallel the dunes. Yes, indeed, fall is a glorious season to be outdoors.

While many people are inclined to be outside on a sunny October's day, not all of us are cut out to use a viewer. You must work slowly with this device. Move too fast and the bottom becomes a big, brown blur. For the less patient, a push net may be a better way to go. This net has a straight front edge which can be angled against the sea floor and pushed through the grass while walking along at a moderate clip. As the lead bar scrapes across the bottom, any scallop it bumps tumbles into the netting behind it. Both scoop and push

Above, divers easily pick scallops from the bottom. At right, a scalloper prepares to work his push net through a dense bed of eelgrass.

nets are constructed of light chain since constant rubbing against the bottom and rough edged scallop shells tend to make quick work of nylon, plastic or cotton mesh.

If there's a catch to scalloping, it has to be that these shellfish are reliably unreliable. Finding the motherlode one Saturday in no way ensures a good catch the following weekend. Because it can freely move about, the scallop does. Always, though, it travels with a purpose: to escape a predator, to find warmer or cooler water, denser cover or better feeding grounds. If you find them one day but not the next, try looking in deeper water or move a few hundred yards in another direction. If need be, scallop schools can migrate more than a quarter mile in a week.

Though there isn't room enough to cover them in detail, there are two other ways to gather scallops that deserve at least a mention. The first is snorkeling or scuba diving. The second is using a scallop dredge. For the diver, the procedure is easy. Simply pick them up off the bottom and place them in your sack. If you want to try a scallop dredge, I suggest you stop and talk with a few commercial baymen. They can tell you where to buy one or, possibly, how to build a small one to drag behind your boat. Be aware that in many states it's illegal to use a dredge of any type without purchasing a commercial license.

It's no secret that bay scallop populations have been on the decline in recent years. Development, pollution and the mysterious brown tide have all taken their toll. Especially distressing has been the slow disappearance of eelgrass from some inland bays, for it is within these underwater fields that the scallop feels most at home. Where the eelgrass has vanished, so too has this pretty shellfish. As such, you can expect scalloping regulations and seasons to be strictly enforced in most localities with restrictions on the methods of harvest, net size, etc. quite varied from state to state or even town to town.

Because there aren't always enough to go around, scallops are unlikely to ever become as popular among recreational clammers as are clams, mussels or oysters. But then, perhaps that's fitting. If the sea were nothing but a big shopping mall, those other three might be found on the shelves of most any major department store. The scallop would be found only at Fortunoff's.

Five

EDIBLE EXTRAS

*O*ne of the most pleasing aspects of shell-fishing lies in the knowledge that anywhere clams, oysters, mussels or scallops abound, so do other tasty morsels. Scungilli, moon snails, razor clams and the like are special treats, usually unexpected but always welcomed to grace a plate. I like to refer to these sidelights as "edible extras", for few clammers ever head out with them specifically in mind. Somehow, though, most find a couple in their basket by the end of the day.

Following is a brief synopsis of several popular "extras" you may encounter from time to time on your clamming forays.

SCUNGILLI

Technically, these are called whelks — but then whoever claimed to have eaten a whelk salad or linguini with whelk and hot sauce?

Actually, there are several kinds of edible whelks to be found along our shores. The two most common are the knobbed and channel whelks, each of which fosters several more monickers such as "northern conch", "sea snail" or "winkle". Both species grow to about ten inches in length with a thick-walled, spiral-shaped shell that when empty fits comfortably over a man's hand. Hold it to your ear and listen to the ocean surf tumbling inside. Knobbed whelks are found primarily in the northern and temperate waters while channel whelks prefer the warmer currents of the southern and gulf coasts.

The spiral shaped shells of these two creatures are very similar in appearance, the main difference being the knobbed points on the spiral  lines of the northern variety. The southern dweller is relatively smooth. Both exhibit a light brown, tan, or dull yellowish-white outside shell with an interior that is typically pale yellow, peach or orange. (True conch, for comparison, live only in tropical waters and possess a bright pink interior shell.)

As any scungilli lover would have you know, the entire meat of this shellfish is edible. It is easily removed from the shell with a fork after five to ten minutes of boiling or steaming. Most people discard the spongy viscera that is noticeable after slicing the meat in half — and just about everyone slices off the tough "foot" section. This huge snail has a chewy texture that I truly enjoy. For those who like their meat a little more tender, pounding, grinding or marinating each add a different degree of softness.

Scungilli can be sliced and served with butter sauce, hot sauce, spaghetti or linguini. It also makes for great clam fritters and chowders. Served cold, it is splendid in a salad.

SURF CLAMS

I like the name "skimmer clams" better, as the word "surf" seems a bit deceptive here. The name surf clam comes from the fact that their somewhat triangular shaped shells frequently wash up in the suds along ocean beaches. Their brittle coverings could never stand up to a pounding surf, however, for they are only slightly more thick-walled than steamers. Hence, they tend to colonize outside the breakers. While most people associate  surf clams strictly with ocean waters, they also thrive inside salty bays and estuaries where they are harvested in the same manner as hard clams.

Although skimmers may grow very large, sometimes reaching more than eight inches across the shell, they are particularly good eating. Slightly tougher and stronger tasting than softshells or quahogs, they are ideal for making chowders, stews, deep fried clam strips, fritters or baked clams. In fact, it is this clam which many restaurents use in their clam strip recipes.

Should you be fortunate enough to shuck some live skimmers, be sure to cut out and place the adductor muscles aside for yourself. They are quite large and can be enjoyed just like bay scallops.

RAZOR CLAMS

This is an interesting creature which commonly inhabits the same flats as steamer and hard clams, though it lives in depths of up to 120 feet.

Razor clams are aptly named for their shells grow long and thin and are square at both ends

Hold one across the palm of your hand and it looks amazingly like an old-fashioned straight razor, the kind which now seems to exist only at authentic barber shops. Though usually measuring five or six inches long, they may grow to be 10 inches or more.

Like the steamer, razor clams are mobile and it's a curious sight to watch them burrow into the sediment. Usually, you'll spot one sticking half-way out of the mud. As you approach it, however, a strong, muscular foot that may be as long as the shell itself is already preparing to suck it underground. One heavy step and, quick as a wink, the razor disappears into the bottom. If you try to get it, you'd better make the first scoop count for it moves quickly under the surface and gatherers rarely ever catch one that's been given a good head start.

Razor clams feature a creamy colored, sweet tasting meat that is delicious when steamed and served with drawn butter. They can also be fried or added to chowder and stews, though it's rare that you'll catch more than a couple on any one outing.

PERIWINKLES

These are close cousins to the whelks but they come much smaller. In fact, their brown, black or olive colored spiraled shells rarely ever grow to be more than an inch across. Because of this, it takes a lot of peris to make a meal. Usually, they end up in some kind of marinara sauce or salad, though I've also heard that they are served with melted butter and toast. Generally, periwinkles are steamed or boiled and a toothpick used to work each meat free from its tiny shell.

These little snails are a common shoreline sight, clinging to piers, rocks, bulkheads and bridge abutments within the intertidal zone and feeding on the algae these structures support. From what I've read, they are a fairly recent immigrant to the new world, coming across the ocean from Europe by hitch-hiking on boat bottoms within the past 100 years. Because they are tolerant of turbid and even slightly polluted water, it is vital that you be sure to pick them only from certified areas.

MOON SNAILS

Like the scungilli, the moon snail or "cockle" is a univalve shellfish which preys mostly on bivalve mollusks. It is particularly fond of quahogs and steamers. Ashy-brown to brown in color, this snail may grow to be three inches tall, though usually it is about one and a half to two inches high. Adult moon snails may eat as many as five cherrystone clams a week and, if necessary, they will dig as deep as three or four inches to find their prey. Steamer gatherers usually spot them lying along the seaside edge of the low water mark where they can be gathered by hand. Like scungilli, moon snails are usually boiled or steamed and require a bit of tenderizing. Their discarded shells are a favorite residence of large hermit crabs.

SEA URCHINS

I have to honestly say that I've never consumed any part of a sea urchin, though several Sea Grant publications assure that the roe from this spiney organism is quite edible. The most common in-shore species is the green sea urchin, known to inhabit tidal pools, reefs and rocky shoreline sections of both the east and west coast. While it can be gathered from the intertidal zone, it is usually taken by divers in ten to forty feet of water. The roe is served up sushi style or on a cracker with lemon juice. It can also be cooked using any standard roe recipe.

ABALONE

Although there are more than 100 species of abalone, only eight are found in our waters and all of these show up along the west coast. Two species are taken most often, the red abalone and the black abalone. Both, like sea urchins, are usually caught by divers.

A univalve shellfish shaped like a big, human ear, the abalone may reach twelve inches across and weigh eight pounds. Its ivory colored meat has a chewy texture and is often tenderized with a mallet. Like clams and scallops, abalone require very little cooking time and they're frequently sliced and served raw. When cleaned, abalone shells are stunningly pretty, flashing hues of ir-ridescent blue, green, red and pink across their silky inside sheen when struck by sunshine. They make for beautiful and interesting coffee table adornments.

Chapter 6
FINDING SHELLFISH BEDS

*N*ow that you have a little background info under your belt about shellfish ways and habitat requirements, where can you go to legally gather a few? This is often the crux of the matter for the successful clammer as attaining access to good habitat along some parts of the coast can be a chore. With a little effort and research, though, it's almost always possible to find at least a couple of close-by gathering grounds if you live near or visit the shore. Despite being overdeveloped in most coastal states, our seashore and its backwater stretches constitute thousands of miles, a good deal of it protected in the form of state, federal, county or local parks open to the public. Beginning and even experienced clammers can make use of these, and often the clamming will be good and the entrance fees small.

Just imagine how rich with sea life the bottom might be within the boundaries of a Federal Wilderness area that blankets several miles of a barrier island, yet provides access only by foot trail? Or, think of the acres and acres of productive marsh that line intercoastal waterways like Barnegat Bay or Chincoteague Bay. Here, all kinds of tasty morsels can be gathered while coot, brant, geese and sea ducks cruise by. Then too, there is the National Seashore, which quite often has a back bay border all but ignored by the throngs of ocean loving sun worshipers who scatter their bodies across the thin ribbons of sand up front. Let's hope they stay on their blankets for it is here, on the quiet backwaters, away from the crowds, that buckets are filled most quickly. It's very rare that good shellfishing is found along the ocean side. Each and every coastal state, by the way, can boast of having federal or state wetlands where shellfishing is permitted or even encouraged — a thought to put your mind a little more at ease as you pass by the "Private Beach" and "No Parking" signs which seem more numerous than the clams you'll catch in some developed coastal stretches.

Before getting started in your clamming endeavors, you'll need to find out if a permit is required for the area in which you'll be prospecting. This requires a trip, or at least a phone call, to the appropriate agency to speak with those in charge of shellfishing. As long as you're going to make that much effort anyway, you might as well go a step further and try to dig up a little "where to" information.

Shellfish regulatory agencies vary from state to state and, depending on where you live, it may be the state itself, county, or town that makes local policy. In some areas, all three levels of government have their hands in the pie. It's probably best, then, to start your inquiries at the state level. That's where the broadest rules will apply. While counties and towns may set individual guidelines to govern waters under their own jurisdiction, these will usually deal with where and when you can clam. The how and how much is almost always determined by the state.

In most instances, shellfish regulatory agencies fall under the umbrella of the State Department of Environmental Conservation, Department of Health, or Food and Drug Administration. Further, each state seems to have a different name for the same basic office. Whatever the title, these offices are all charged with the task of ensuring that any shellfish gathered come from, "certified", clean waters and are safe to eat. To do this, the agencies regularly monitor the levels of coliform bacteria. Although this organism isn't a problem itself, it thrives under the same conditions as many harmful bacteria. Since it's relatively easy to sample, it is used as an indicator of possible contamination. Any areas deemed to have excessively high counts of coliform are immediately closed.

In addition to inquiries at the state level, you can also stop by Town Hall or the County Office Building to find out more about local shellfishing possibilities. In general, I've found less satisfaction at this level, but I've still culled enough information to make the effort worthwhile. If nothing else, with a little gentle prodding those dispensing information at the county and town levels can usually refer you to more local organizations along the lines of the Parks and Recreation Departments, Tourism Boards, Chambers of Commerce, Littoral Societies, and even commercial Baymen's Associations. Some of these groups can be a really big help.

Once you've gotten a few leads from the above sources, it's time to do a little scouting, the same kind that fishermen and hunters consider essential. Grab yourself a road atlas and whatever maps or directions you've obtained, and start driving. You'll want to dedicate enough time to this task to allow inspection of several possible locations. I like to take the whole family along, combining this activity with a trip to the beach or a simple and relaxing drive along the shore. In any case, it helps if you can plan your scouting trips to coincide with low tide since that's the time you'll be doing the most clamming. Visit each area you think you might like to try and scope out the situation. Get out and look around, and maybe do a little experimental digging. What kind of shellfish are most prevalent? Are there areas where several species mix? How about other clammers; are they having a good day? Do the grounds seem overworked or overlooked? These are the type of questions you should be asking yourself. Before you leave to check out the next area, look carefully to see which stretches seem most fertile and chart them on your map. Note also the location of jetties, partially submerged rocks and boulders, sandbars, drop-offs and mudflat edges that won't be visible when the tide rolls in. Making a few notes now might might save you a lot of time and wasted effort down the road.

After you've scouted and sampled the shellfishing at a few different public locations, you'll probably begin looking for more secluded and wild areas to try your luck. This seems to be a natural extension of the desire to be outdoors — escaping from the crowds, exploring new territories and just being out on your own. Exploring nearby beaches, ones close enough to the public grounds that they should hold the same type shellfish, is a simple means of getting away. Examine your road atlas for shore access points adjacent to the public grounds and stop to check each one. The backside of a point that serves as a border between state and county lands, a small cove a half-mile down the coast, or town beaches are all possibilities. Frequently, you'll be rebuked by "No Parking" or "Private Beach" signs, but every now and then it's possible to turn up a new spot where no one seems to mind if a small family stops by to gather dinner. Occasionally, you'll stumble across a clammer or two already in the water. End of search if they have full baskets.

From time to time you might spy a stretch of beach that looks particularly inviting but is inaccessible due to coastal development. In such cases, it might be possible to get permission from a homeowner to pass across to the shore. Here, the bribe of "leaving a few behind" can be a great bargaining chip. With a little imagination, it's possible to find a lot of different places to shellfish. Just keep in mind that it isn't worth the effort to clam in areas where you aren't welcome. If the threat of a parking ticket looms, or local residents are going to give you a hard time, you're probably better off going someplace else where you can better enjoy yourself. That's one reason why parklands are so alluring.

Of course, it should be noted that not all clamming is done from the beach. A great way to leave behind the crowds and work more virgin territory is to use a boat to reach flats and sandbars inaccessible to waders. In calm, protected waters, many clammers put to use small inflatable rafts, car-top rowboats or even canoes. These are ideal for crossing channels inside harbors or in back bay locations where even at low tide four to six foot depths may separate the shore from an inviting sandbar or mudflat.

If you're lucky enough to own a larger boat you can probably reach more open water areas where commercial clammers harvest hard clams, mussels and oysters. In the waters off Maine and Massachusetts, for example, there are vast offshore mussel beds that waders never reach. New York, New Jersey, Maryland, Virginia, Delaware, the Carolinas, Louisiana, California and Washington state all have bays and harbors where clams can be gathered at almost any depth to thirty feet — so long as the proper gear is employed. Oftentimes, open waters contain vast flats that can't even be seen from shore, rising up at mid-bay but never fully exposing themselves. Such areas can be waded and clammed just like the shore spots if you have the means of reaching them.

As I mentioned earlier, clamming can be combined with other activities to produce some great trips — especially if you're familiar with local waters. Here's a classic example. Several years ago, a friend visiting for the weekend told me he would like to go clamming *and* fishing. Unfortunately, we had only one day to hit the water. To go clamming or to try for summer flounder then became the dilemma. The solution? We rented a skiff on a local bay and decided to fluke away the morning's dropping tide. As the current slacked off and the fishing died around noontime, we pulled up alongside a series of small sandbars that

I had worked in the past. There we dug two pailfulls of tasty quahogs in about an hour and a half. By the time our buckets were full of littlenecks and cherrystones, the tide was on the rise and we could see the fishing fleet once again lifting flatties into their boats. We pushed off and resumed fishing, quitting around 4 p.m. with about 15 delicious fluke in the cooler and almost a hundred clams to complement our fillets.

STOP! . . . if you see this sign or anything like it. Shellfish should never be taken from "closed" or "uncertified" waters. If you are not sure that an area is safe to clam, pass it by. Note too that "No Shellfishing" signs can take many forms and often vary from town to town.

As you can see, there really are a lot of possibilities when it comes to finding productive shellfishing grounds. In fact, your access is limited more by your own imagination and persistence than by rules, regulations or "No Trespassing" signs. Keep in mind, though, that while some shellfishing grounds are clearly posted as to whether they are safe, it still pays to be careful. Make it a point to avoid working tidal creeks or rivermouths that see heavy boating traffic, flow past garbage dumps or poultry farms, or empty out below a major municipality. You might also abstain from clamming anywhere following a hard rain, as heavy sewage overflow and runoff can significantly raise bacteria levels and deposit alarming amounts of fecal matter in what normally would be considered safe, clean waters.

A LISTING OF STATE SHELLFISH REGULATORY AGENCIES

ALABAMA:
DEC, Div. of Marine
Resources
P.O. Box 189
Dauphin Island, AL
36528

ALASKA:
Dept. of Fish and Game
P.O. Box 3-2000
Juneau, AK 99802

CALIFORNIA:
Dept. of Fish and
Game
Div. of Marine
Resources
1416 Ninth Street
Sacramento, CA 95814

CONN:
DEP, Marine Fisheries
Great Neck Rd.
Waterford, CT 06385

DELAWARE:
Div. of Fish & Wildlife
P.O. Box 1401
Dover, DE 11903

FLORIDA:
Shellfish Admin.
Dept. of Natural
Resources
3900 Commonwealth
Blvd.
Tallahassee, FL 32399

GEORGIA:
Coastal Resources Div.
1200 Glynn Ave.
Brunswick, Georgia
31523-8600

LOUISIANA:
Dept. of Wildlife and
Fisheries
P.O. Box 98000

Baton Rouge, LA
70895

MARYLAND:
Dept. of Natural
Resources
Tawes State Office
Building
Annapolis, MD 21401

MASS:
Div. of Marine Fisheries
100 Cambridge St.
— 19th Floor
Boston, MA 02202

MAINE
Dept. of Marine
Resources
State House
Station #21
Augusta, ME 04333

MISSISSIPPI:
Bureau of Marine
Fisheries
2620 Beach Blvd.
Biloxi, MS 39531

NC:
Div. of Marine Fisheries
3411 Arendell Dr.
Moorehead City, NC
28557

NEW HAMPSHIRE
Dept. of Marine
Resources
Inland and Marine
Fisheries
2 Hazen Dr.
Concord, NH 03301

NJ:
DEP, Bureau of
Shellfisheries
401 East State St.,
Trenton, NJ 08625

NEW YORK:
NYS DEC,
Bureau of
Shellfisheries
Building 40, SUNY
Stony Brook, NY
11794

OREGON:
Dept. of Fish and
Wildlife
P.O. Box 59
Portland, OR 97207

RHODE ISLAND:
Div. of Fish & Wildlife
Washington Cty. Gov't.
Center
Tower Hill Rd.
Wakefield, RI 02879

SC:
Dept. of Fish & Wildlife
Marine Resources Div.
P.O. Box 12559
Charleston, SC 29412

TEXAS:
Texas Parks and
Wildlife Dept.
Coastal Fisheries Div.
4200 Smith School Rd.
Austin, TX 78744

VIRGINIA:
Virginia Resources
Comm.
2401 Washington Ave.
Newport News, VA
23607

WASHINGTON:
Dept. of Fisheries
115 General Admission
Building
Olympia, WA 98504

Seven

STORING
AND CLEANING
YOUR CATCH

*A*s with any food that comes from the sea, proper handling from the time of capture to the moment it graces your plate is essential to ensure a good tasting, healthy meal. Eaten fresh, clams, mussels, oysters, scallops and all the edible extras we've discussed are tasty, low in cholesterol, low in fat and rich in protein. The idea is to keep them that way until they can be served.

Proper shellfish care starts the second you lift your prize from the water. Each captive should be thoroughly washed on the spot to rid its surface of sand, grit, mud or weed growth. It should then be placed in a basket, bag or pail, and kept moist and out of the sun. When you get home, place them in the refrigerator or a cool, dark corner of the garage. Never let any shellfish sit for a prolonged period of time in standing water as they might use up all the oxygen and suffocate. Leaving your catch submerged in plain freshwater is another way to ensure it dies.

If simply kept moist, hardshell clams and oysters can live in your refrigerator for seven to ten days provided the temperature is set between 32 and 35 degrees. Mussels, steamers and scallops are good for only two or three days. (Do not debeard mussels until you are ready to cook them. Doing so tears the meat slightly, leaving them prone to bacterial invasion.) While it's OK to place most shellfish on ice, they shouldn't be buried in it.

Have you ever brought home a basket of shellfish only to find they tasted muddy or contained grains of fine grit or sand? Disappointing isn't it? Well, believe it or not, there's a surefire cure for this condition. Just place your oysters, clams or mussels in a bucket filled with clean, freshwater. To to each gallon of H2O mix in one cup of salt and a cup of yellow cornmeal. Within a few minutes, your dinner-to-be should begin feeding in the brine solution, pumping out the grit and mud and filling up on cornmeal. In about two hour's time, the cornmeal will even replace the green or black contents to be found in their stomachs. This should make your catch more pleasing to the squeamish. Be sure to change the brine solution every twenty minutes or so to replenish the oxygen.

One concern that might arise as you examine the day's catch is the discovery of unwanted extras. Small worms will occasionally show up in clams or oysters and the tiny pea crab is frequently found residing inside blue mussels during the summertime. Naturally, you'll want to discard any infested shellfish you come across, but you'll be glad to know that no harm will come to you should a few be missed.

Before you eat any shellfish, raw or cooked,

always ask yourself this one vital question: *Did it come from certified waters?*

If you can't answer the query honestly, don't even think about putting it in your mouth. The mistake could prove sickening — or even fatal.

Although you've already culled your catch by the time you're ready to open or cook it, a final check is still in order before you commit to supper. Hard clams, oysters and mussels should be tightly closed or able to shut when gently tapped on a countertop. The shells should not be cracked or otherwise damaged to the point where the meat might contact outside bacteria. Oysters should have one well cupped shell while steamers should be able to contract their necks when prodded. Scallop meats must smell sweet and be firm in texture. If the shell of any clam, mussel, scallop or oyster can be pried apart by hand, throw the critter out. It's dead or dying.

While I don't know of anyone who really enjoys opening shellfish, I have seen quite a few baymen take pride in doing it right. Some, in fact, seem to find great pleasure in watching a novice try to open a clam (or better yet, scallop or oyster) for the first time. For the beginner, separating the meats from their shells can be shear torture. Clams, oysters and scallops, the three mollusks most often eaten raw, are especially stubborn and without some knowledge of how to proceed one might conclude smashing them open is the only logical solution. Even that won't end your frustration, though, for doing so doesn't leave the meat in a recognizable form.

Every shellfish gatherer should learn the proper methods of parting these three. The following procedures and accompanying illustrations should get you started. Using the appropriate utensils will help, too. Before you begin, let me offer this one small tip: 10 minutes in the freezer, sixty seconds in a microwave, or two minutes over a steampot is usually enough to relax the muscles of most shellfish without freezing or cooking the meats. While the expert doesn't need the extra edge, many beginners find this tactic makes shucking a much simpler task. Those shellfish not mentioned below can usually be steamed or boiled open. Use a lobster fork or toothpick to pull the meats from their shells.

SHUCKING HARD CLAMS

1. Hold the clam in the crook of your palm with the top of its hinge facing the base of your thumb and the heart-shaped

side pointing toward your index finger. To anchor the clam in place, put your thumb over the top shell. To keep the juice from spilling out, hold the clam parallel to the floor for the following steps.

2. Align the sharp edge of a clam knife with the seam between the two shells. Pressing against the dull edge of the knife blade with your fingertips, force the blade between the shells.

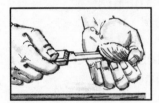

3. Once inserted, twist the blade slightly to pry the shells apart about a quarter of an inch. Insert a fingertip between the shells to wedge them open.

4. Carefully work the knife along the inside of the top shell, severing the two adductor muscles which hold the shells together as you separate the meat.

5. Flip off the top shell and loosen the clam from its lower shell by smoothly running the

blade under the meat and severing the lower adductors. Remove any visible shell fragments that you come across. This same procedure will also work on skimmer and soft shelled clams, both of which are easier to open as their shells do not close so tightly.

Tips: Stubborn clams can be weakened by working the knife blade into the hinge at the top (point) of the clam. Press the knife as hard as you can between the hinge and upper shell. Wiggle the blade up and down several times until you feel the clam begin to loosen up. Proceed as above.

SHUCKING OYSTERS

1. Place the oyster flat on a table and hold it down from the wide end. Oysters have a rounded top and flat bottom shell. To keep the juice from flowing out as they are opened, you need to hold them upside down. In other words, the rounded shell should always be on the bottom.

2. Insert the tip of an oyster knife into the hinge at the front (pointed end) of the oyster where the two shells connect. You should feel the tip "bite" into the hinge.

3. Holding the oyster in place, twist the knife blade at a right angle to the table. The shells should "pop" slightly apart.

4. Work the blade along the flat shell, severing the meat and cutting the adductor muscles. The flat edge of the blade should run against the shell, the raised edge against the meat.

5. Flip off the flat shell and loosen the meat from the rounded shell. If you wish to save the juice, drain it through cheesecloth and into a pot or bowl.

Tips: Oyster shells often have sharp edges. Wear a glove on the hand that will be used to hold them in place.

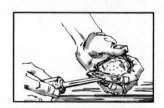

SHUCKING SCALLOPS

1. Position the scallop in the crook of your palm with the hinged end facing your thumb and the cleaner shell against your hand. Place your thumb on top of the shell to secure.

2. Insert a scallop or clam knife between the shells at the slight opening just below the "wings".

3. Twist the knife to lift the top shell slightly. Do not force the shells open as the adductor muscle may tear.

4. Place a fingertip between the shells to wedge them apart and slide the knife inside along the top shell just behind the hinge. Cut the adductor and flip the top shell off.

5. Leaving the marshmallow-like adductor attached to the bottom shell, gently remove and discard the viscera (soft body) by pinching it between the knife blade and a finger. If present, the orange colored roe may be retained and eaten.

6. Cut the adductor from the bottom shell. Usually, only this part of the scallop is eaten.

Tips: Scallops require a gentle touch. Force them open and the meat will tear or the shell might crack. Because the shells are rough edged, wear a glove on the hand which holds this shellfish in place, or wrap some electrical tape across your palm between your thumb and index finger.

Eight
DELICIOUS SHELLFISH RECIPES

C atching shellfish is a lot of fun but eating them is what gets most coast strollers excited. Fortunately for the clammer, these tasty treats are generally easy to cook and healthy to eat. There are two rules to keep in mind when cooking shellfish of any kind, however: 1) Don't overcook them, and 2) Use recipes that enhance, not hide, their true seaside flavor.

Most shellfish can be eaten raw. They can also be fried or steamed and for these cooking methods it seems that almost everybody has an old family recipe. Following, though, are a few that I consider superior to the standard means of preparation. I hope you'll enjoy them as much as I do.

APPETIZERS AND HORS D'OEUVRES

HALFSHELL MUSSEL DELIGHT
Blend 1 tsp. curry or favorite spice blend per half cup of mayonnaise and chill. Dip chilled, steamed mussel meats in mayonnaise mix and return to shell. Serve cold.

BROILED SCALLOP APPETIZERS

1 dozen scallop meats
2 egg yolks — beaten
1 T. lemon juice

6 strips bacon cut in half
Dash paprika
Parsley for garnish

Mix lemon juice and beaten egg yolks in dish. Dip each scallop into egg mixture, then wrap one-half bacon strip around each. Secure with toothpick. Place on broiler pan three inches from heat for four minutes. Turn each scallop once. Garnish with paprika and parsley. Serve at once. Serves 2.

STUFFED CLAMS

1 cup minced clams with
  juice
1 cup cubed or shredded
  bread
1 tsp. minced onion
Paprika

1 tsp. chopped celery
Dash of tabasco
Grated Parmesan cheese
1/4 tsp. Worcestershire
  sauce

Mix clams and bread. Add onion, celery, Worcestershire and tabasco. Spoon into shells and sprinkle cheese on top. Bake in oven at 350 degrees for ten minutes. Add dashes of paprika and broil until top is crisp.

SHELLFISH VINAIGRETTE

1/2 cup olive oil
1/4 cup white vinegar
1 tsp. oregano
1 tsp. basil

1 tsp. parsley
1/2 tsp. black pepper
Salt to taste

Combine and blend all ingredients well and chill. Drizzle onto cooked and cooled shellfish. Clams, mussels and scallops work best. Serve with toothpicks.

MUSSEL COCKTAIL

36 mussels   1/2 cup dry white wine
1 bay leaf   1/4 cup chopped onion

In large pot, place white wine, bay leaf and onion. Bring to boil. Add mussels, cover and cook over high heat until shells open. Remove mussels from shells and place in a mixing bowl. Cover and refrigerate until serving time.

Dressing:

Lettuce for lining serving bowls   1/2 cup chopped celery
1 cup mayonnaise   1/4 T. salt
1 hard-cooked egg, chopped   1/4 tsp. black pepper
2 T. lemon juice   1 T. gin (optional)
Chopped parsley   Lemon wedges

Mix mayonnaise, egg, lemon juice, celery, salt, pepper and gin together. Fold mussels into dressing. Divide mussels among lettuce-lined bowls according to servings needed. Sprinkle with chopped parsley.

HERBED YOGURT DIPPING SAUCE

1/2 egg yolk   2 garlic cloves — minced
1 egg white   1 1/2 T. lime juice
2 T. safflower oil   1 T. dijon mustard
1 T. olive oil   1/8 tsp. salt
1/2 cup plain yogurt   Dash black pepper
2 T. green onions — finely   1 T. finely chopped fresh
    chopped   basil, parsley or dill

Place egg yolk and egg white in large bowl. Whisking vigorously, pour safflower oil into bowl in a fine steady stream. Add olive oil the same way. Whisk in yogurt, onions, garlic, lime juice, mustard, salt, pepper and spice. Refrigerate for at least 20 minutes. Use on fresh raw oysters, clams or mussels.

TOM'S SPICY COCKTAIL SAUCE

1 cup catsup	Dash celery salt
3 T. white horseradish	5-7 drops tabasco sauce
Dash garlic salt	1 tsp. fresh lemon juice

Mix together all ingredients and stir thoroughly. Chill at least 1/2 hour before serving on raw or fried oysters, scallops or clams.

CLAM AND CHEESE DIP

1 cup minced, cooked clams of any type	1 tsp. Worcestershire sauce
2 pkgs. (3 oz.) cream cheese	3-4 drops tabasco sauce
2 tsp. lemon juice	1/4 tsp. salt
2 tsp. grated onions	1 tsp. minced parsley

Soften cream cheese at room temperature. Combine all ingredients and blend into a paste. Chill and serve with assorted chips and crackers.

RED WINE DIPPING SAUCE

3 cups red wine	1 tsp. fresh thyme
2 cloves garlic — minced	or 1/4 tsp. dried thyme
2 T. chopped shallot	2 tsp. honey
1 1/2 T. lemon juice	1/8 tsp. salt
Black pepper to taste	

Pour wine into porcelain saucepan over medium heat. Cook wine until reduced to one cup — about 20 minutes. Add garlic, shallot, lemon juice, thyme, honey, salt and pepper and cook for ten minutes. Refrigerate for 45 minutes. Use with fresh raw oysters, clams, or mussels.

GRILLED OYSTERS

24 oysters in shell
Lemon wedges and/or dipping sauce

Place oysters, rounded shell down, on ungreased grill 4-6 inches from coals. Cover with lid or aluminum foil tent. Cook until oysters begin to open, 3-10 minutes. With an oyster knife, open shells and detach oysters, reserving juice. Serve in shell or return to grill and continue cooking until edges curl slightly. Serve with lemon wedges and a dipping sauce if desired.

GRILLED MUSSELS OR CLAMS

For each appetizer serving, place 8 to 12 mussels or six clams on a rectangle of heavy duty foil. Add 1 T. white wine and 1/8 tsp. thyme to each packet. Seal and place on grill for 5 minutes or until shellfish opens. Each packet makes one appetizer.

SOUPS AND SALADS

CLAM & MACARONI SALAD

Simply add cooled, chopped, cooked clams to macaroni salad. Very delicious.

MUSSEL STUFFED TOMATOES

4 large ripe tomatoes
2 cups cooked, chopped and
   drained mussel meats
4 black olives
Italian dressing
Salt and pepper to taste

4 tsp. chopped green onion
1 cup chopped celery
Loose lettuce (Boston)
2 cups small curd cottage
   cheese

Cut off tomato tops. Gently spoon out seeds and discard. Combine mussels, cottage cheese, onion and celery. Fill tomato shells. Line salad plates with lettuce, place tomato on each and top with olive. Serve with Italian dressing. Serves 4.

OYSTER STEW

1 pint shucked oysters
2 cups milk
1 cup light cream
Dash bottled hot pepper
   sauce (optional)

Paprika
Butter or margarine
Parsley
Salt & pepper

In a medium saucepan combine the undrained oysters and 3/4 tsp. salt. Cook over medium heat about five minutes or till edges of oysters curl. Stir in milk, cream and hot pepper sauce. Heat through. Season to taste with additional salt and pepper. Sprinkle each serving with paprika and parsley and top with a pat of butter or margarine. Serves 4.

OYSTER AND MUSSEL PASTA DELIGHT

1 dozen shucked oysters,
   save juice
2 pounds mussels, scrubbed
   and debearded
1 cup Italian-style salad
   dressing
6 ozs. uncooked spiral pasta

1/2 cup each red bell
   pepper strips, thinly
   sliced carrot, sliced
   mushrooms, broccoli
   florets and thawed
   frozen peas
1/4 cup chopped parsley

Simmer oysters in their juice (or clam juice) 3-5 minutes over low heat until edges begin to curl. Drain. Place mussels in large kettle with 3/4 cup boiling water. Cover and steam over moderate heat for 2-3 minutes until shells open. Combine mussel meats with oysters and salad dressing. Refrigerate overnight. Two hours before serving, cook pasta. Drain oysters and mussels, reserving dressing. In large bowl, combine hot pasta with reserved dressing and let stand for 15 minutes. Stir in oysters, mussels and vegetables. Refrigerate 2 hours or more before serving.

MUSSEL BISQUE

3 T. butter	1 cup milk and 1 cup cream
2 egg yolks — well beaten	1 tsp. lemon juice
2 T. minced green onions	1/2 tsp. paprika
1 cup mussel meat	Salt & pepper to taste
1 cup mussel broth saved	Sour cream
from steaming	Parsley

Very lightly saute onion in butter until onion is soft. In a saucepan, combine onion, mussels, broth, milk, cream and lemon juice. Heat. Add a little of this to egg yolks and blend immediately; stir slowly back into soup. Add paprika, salt and pepper while stirring. Warm until just hot enough to serve. Garnish with dollops of sour cream and parsley.

MANHATTAN CLAM CHOWDER (Red)

1 pint chopped hard clams	1 tsp. basil
1/2 cup chopped celery	1 tsp. thyme
1/2 cup chopped carrot	1 tsp. parsley
2 medium potatoes	1 bay leaf
— diced and peeled	1 T. vegetable oil
1 28 oz. can crushed tomatoes	1 tsp. oregano
3 cups clam broth	Salt and pepper to taste

In a large pot or dutch oven, lightly saute onion. Drain. Add tomatoes, broth, celery, oregano, basil, thyme, parsley, salt, pepper and bay leaf. Simmer on low heat 15 minutes. Add carrots, potatoes and water and bring to boil. Lower heat and simmer 35 minutes. Add clams and heat through.

SCALLOP STEW

1 T. butter
1/2 cup red bell pepper
  (diced)
1 scallion (diced)
1 cup half-and-half
1/2 tsp. crushed, dried
  thyme
Dash cayenne pepper

1 T. tomato paste
1 medium potato (peeled
  and diced)
1/2 pound scallops
1/4 cup scallop juice
  or clam broth
Salt and white pepper

Melt butter in a medium saucepan, add bell pepper and scallion. Saute over low to medium heat for approximately 5 minutes. Add half-and-half, thyme, cayenne and tomato paste. Simmer 2-3 minutes but do not boil. Add potato and scallops and simmer 5 minutes. Season lightly with salt and pepper.

NEW ENGLAND CLAM CHOWDER (White)

2 T. flour
1/2 cup onion (diced)
1/2 cup celery
1 pound chopped clams
2 cups light cream
2 cups milk
1 T. parsley
1 1/2 cups clam juice

2 T. butter
1 cup potatoes pared
  and diced
1/2 tsp. salt
1/2 tsp. thyme
3 or 4 drops tabasco sauce
1/4 tsp. white pepper

Heat butter in large skillet or saucepan. Add onion and celery and cook slowly until tender. Blend flour into this and cook over low heat for three minutes. Scald cream and milk, then stir into vegetables gradually. Add potatoes, clam juice and spices. Bring mixture to a slow boil, reduce heat, cover and cook for 30 minutes, stirring frequently. Add chopped clams and heat through. Sprinkle with parsley and serve with oyster crackers or saltines.

MAIN COURSES

OYSTER LOAF

1 pint oysters	2 loaves French or Italian
1/2 tsp. salt	bread 15 X 3 inches
1/8 tsp. pepper	Fat for deep frying
2 eggs — beaten	1/2 cup tartar sauce
1/4 cup milk	1 1/2 cups shredded
3/4 cup flour	lettuce
2 cups bread crumbs	15 thin tomato slices
1/2 cup melted butter or margarine	

Shuck oysters and pat dry. Sprinkle with salt and pepper. Combine milk and eggs. Roll oysters in flour, dip into egg mixture then roll in bread crumbs. Refrigerate at least 30 minutes. Slice bread loaves in half horizontally. Pull out the inside soft part from bottom and top halves of bread. Brush the bread shells inside with melted butter or margarine. Place bread shells on baking sheet and bake in moderate oven at 350 degrees for three to five minutes till warm and crisp.

Place oysters in a single layer in a fry basket. Fry in deep fat at 350 degrees for two to three minutes. Drain on absorbent paper. Spread inside of bread slices with tartar sauce. Place shredded lettuce in the bottom halves of the loaves. Arrange tomato slices on top of lettuce, and fried oysters on top of tomatoes. Cover with top halves of the loaves of bread. Cut each loaf into three portions. Serves 6.

BACON-SADDLED SCALLOPS

1 lb. shucked bay scallops	5-6 slices bacon
1/4 cup French dressing	

Broil bacon slightly; cut in 2 inch pieces. Dip scallops in dressing and wrap with bacon piece, secure with toothpick. Arrange on skewers, 1/2 inch apart. Place on broiling pan and broil 2-3 inches from heat 5-7 minutes until bacon is crisp. Turn halfway through. Push scallops off skewers to serve.

CURRIED STEAMERS

4 dozen shucked, cooked
   steamers
2 cups milk
1/2 cup heavy cream
2 tsp. curry powder

4 T. flour
2 T. butter
1 onion, minced
1 clove garlic, minced
Dash salt and pepper

Scald milk. In a separate pan, saute onion and garlic in oil.
Add butter. When melted, stir in flour and curry powder until
smooth. Add salt and pepper. Mix in steamer meat, milk and
cream. Serve with rice or noodles. Serves 2 to 4.

FRIED CLAMS, OYSTERS, OR SCALLOPS WITH DILL

2 cups shucked clams,
   oysters or scallops
1/3 cup flour
1/4 tsp. salt
1/4 tsp. pepper

2 eggs beaten
1 cup fine bread crumbs
1 tsp. dried dill
Shortening or cooking oil
   for deep fat frying

Drain clams, oysters or scallops. Gently pat dry with paper
towel. In a shallow bowl stir together flour, salt and pepper.
Roll shellfish in seasoned flour. Dip coated shellfish in a
mixture of beaten eggs and two T. water, then roll in bread
crumb and dill mixture. Fry in deep hot fat (375 degrees) till
golden. Allow one minute for clams, 1 1/2 minutes for
oysters and two minutes for scallops. Serves 4.

CLAM FRITTERS

2 T. butter
1/2 cup onion (diced)
1 tsp. parsley
1 pound potatoes (peeled)
1 pound chopped clams
   with juice

2 egg yolks
1 ounce heavy cream
1/4 tsp. black pepper
1/2 tsp. salt
Cracker meal

Boil potatoes and then mash. Saute onion and parsley in
butter until tender. Beat egg yolks and cream, add pepper,

salt and chopped clams with juice and combine with mashed potatoes to make a semi-stiff dough. Roll out and cut into cakes with biscuit cutter. Coat each side of cakes in cracker meal. Cook in hot oil until golden brown. Serve hot with linguine and red clam sauce, or eat plain with a dash of salt and pepper or tabasco sauce.

SAUTEED SCALLOPS

2 dozen scallops	1 stick butter
1 green onion, chopped	1/2 cup dry white wine
2 cloves garlic, minced	Dash salt and pepper
1 T. lemon juice	

In a skillet, melt butter and add lemon. Add scallops, onion and garlic while stirring constantly. When scallops turn from pink to white, pour wine in and simmer for about six minutes. Serves 2.

MUSSEL OR CLAM HOT SAUCE

1 28 ounce can crushed tomatoes	1 tsp. parsley
1 3 ounce can tomato paste	1 tsp. black pepper
1 medium onion, chopped	1 /4 tsp. red pepper
1 clove garlic, minced	1/2 tsp. tabasco
1 tsp. oregano	1/2 tsp. salt
2 pounds mussels or little neck clams	1 bay leaf
	1 tsp. basil

Combine all ingredients except shellfish. Bring to a boil. Reduce heat and simmer 30 minutes. Add shellfish and cook till open. Serve over spaghetti or linguini. Serves 4 to 6.

OYSTER BENEDICT WITH CAPERS

2 dozen oysters, shucked, retain juice	6 slices white bread
Caper Hollandaise	1 pkg. sliced Canadian-style bacon

Caper Hollandaise:

1 jar (6 ozs.) hollandaise sauce	1 T. drained capers
	2 T. light cream

Combine sauce, cream and capers. Heat, stirring occasionally. Do not boil. Makes approximately 3/4 cup sauce.

Toast bread and place on warm serving platter. Fry bacon in 10-inch skillet. Drain on absorbent paper. Place bacon on toast. Pour oysters and juice (or clam juice) into skillet and simmer 3-5 minutes until edges curl. Remove oysters with a slatted spoon and place on bacon. Pour hot Caper Hollandaise over oysters. Serve immediately.

LITTLE NECK POSSILLIPO

Note: 6 dozen mussels can be substituted for the clams in this recipe, or mussels and clams can be mixed together.

3/4 cup olive oil

3 T. chopped fresh garlic

3 cans (28 oz. each) Italian peeled tomatoes (whole)

1 T. oregano

1 T. salt.

1/2 tsp. black pepper

3 oz. cooking sherry

1/4 tsp. thyme

2 T. fresh chopped parsley

4 dozen little neck clams

Open tomatoes and set aside. In a 6 qt. sauce pan heat olive oil and chopped garlic over high heat until garlic begins to turn golden brown. Immediately add all three cans of tomatoes to prevent the garlic from burning. Adjust heat to very low and stir in oregano, salt and pepper. Let simmer for 2 to 2 1/2 hours, stirring occasionally. Do not let the sauce boil. After 1 1/2 hours, the tomatoes should be soft. Crush the whole pieces into small chunks with a wire whisk and continue simmering for remaining cooking time. In a seperate pot, steam clams open in 12 to 15 ounces of water. Drain off half the liquid in pot, add the sherry and cook 2-3 minutes more. Next, add 6-8 ozs. of sauce for each dozen clams. Cover and simmer 5-8 minutes until clams are tender. To serve: Use tongs or a large spoon to arrange a dozen clams per serving bowl. Spoon sauce over clams and sprinkle a pinch of thyme and fresh parsley over each serving. Serve alongside spaghetti or linguini.

STEAMED MUSSELS WITH WINE SAUCE

3 dozen mussels

1 1/2 cup onion, chopped

1/3 cup butter

2 cups dry white wine

4 T. lemon juice

1/4 cup fresh parsley

2 T. butter

2 T. flour

Scrub and debeard mussels. Soak in cold water for an hour. Melt 1/3 cup butter in a six quart saucepan and saute onion until transparent. Add wine, parsley, lemon juice and mussels. Cover and simmer about eight minutes until mussels open. Remove mussels to a bowl and cover with a damp hot towel. Make a paste of the butter and flour. Add to liquid in saucepan. Stir until thickened. Pour over mussels and serve. Serves 4 to 6.

CLAM PIZZA

CRUST:

2 packages quick rise active dry yeast	1/2 cup vegetable oil
	4 T. olive oil
2 cups warm water	5 1/2 cups flour

In a large bowl dissolve the yeast in the water. Add the oils and three cups of flour. Beat with an electric mixer, (or by hand) for ten minutes. Mix in the additional 2 1/2 cups flour. Knead for several minutes. Fold dough out onto countertop and cover with a large metal bowl. Allow to rise until double. Punch down and let rise again. Punch down again and dough is ready. Makes enough dough for two pies.

FILLING for 9-10 inch oiled cake pan:

1/4 pound sliced mozzarella	1 tsp. parsley
2 cups plum tomatoes slightly crushed and drained	2 cloves garlic, finely minced
1 tsp. basil	1 cup cooked and chopped hard clams
1 tsp. oregano	3 T. olive oil
4 T. grated parmesan cheese	Salt to taste

Spread dough in bottom of pan and push up the sides. Make it 1/8 inch thick throughout the pan. Place cheese in layers on bottom of pie. Next, put in the tomatoes, basil, oregano, parsley, garlic and salt. Add chopped clams and top with grated cheese. Drizzle olive oil over the top. Bake at 475 degrees until top is golden and crust is light brown — about 35-40 minutes. Serves 4 to 8.

MUSSEL CASSEROLE

3 cups cooked and drained mussel meat	1/3 cup grated parmesan cheese
2 tsp. finely chopped onion	1/2 tsp. basil
1 clove garlic, minced	1/2 cup fine bread crumbs
2 T. chopped parsley	1/4 cup melted margarine
1 tsp. paprika	Salt and pepper to taste
1 tsp. oregano	

Butter a wide, shallow baking dish and spread mussels in it. Mix onion, garlic, parsley, paprika, oregano, basil and cheese and sprinkle over mussels. Add salt and pepper. Top with crumbs and drizzle with butter. Bake uncovered in pre-heated 425 degree oven for 20 minutes or until hot and brown. Serves 4.

SEASIDE CLAMBAKE

In sand, scoop a circular hole 3 feet wide by 1 foot deep. Line hole with smooth, round stones and build a fire in the pit. Let stones heat for 2-3 hours. Shovel out hot coals and place a 4 inch layer of moist seaweed in the pit. Spill clams, mussels or oysters over seaweed and add corn, potatoes, lobster, crabs or chicken halves. Cover with 3-4 inches more moist seaweed and a tarp if possible. Allow all to steam for approximately 2 hours, uncover and dig in. For a backyard bake, lava rocks can be used instead of stones.

SOUTHERN STYLE OYSTER ROAST

Like the clambake, oyster roasts are usually held at the beach, although a backyard might serve the purpose nearly as well. Dig a long trench two feet deep by two feet wide. Cover the trench with one or several 8X4 foot sheets of sheet metal supported by stakes driven into the ground at each corner of the trench. The sheet metal sheets should be positioned about 2 1/2 feet above the trench. In the trench build a fire and simply place your oysters on the sheet, allowing them to roast open. Ears of corn, lobster, hotdogs, burgers and even halved chickens can be cooked right along with the shellfish. Be careful, however, that you build the pit so that the flames cannot reach near the edges of the sheet metal.